Sir Francis Drake, "drawn from the life" at age 43.
Engraved by Jodocus Hondius, circa 1587.

By Permission of The British Library

Sir Francis Drake's

Secret Voyage to the
Northwest Coast of America, AD 1579

Samuel Bawlf

Sir Francis Drake Publications

Salt Spring Island
British Columbia

2001

Sir Francis Drake Publications Ltd.
P.O. Box 236
Salt Spring Island
British Columbia, V8K 2V9

National Library of Canada Cataloguing in Publication Data

Bawlf, R. Samuel

    Sir Francis Drake's secret voyage to the northwest coast of America, AD 1579

    Includes bibliographical references

    ISBN 0-9688528 – 0 – 7

    1. Drake, Francis, Sir, 1540? – 1596. 2. Northwest Coast of North America – Discovery and exploration – British. 3. Northwest Coast of North America – Maps. 4. Northwest Coast of North America – History – 16th century. 5. Great Britain – History, Naval – Tudors, 1485 – 1603. I. Title.

DA86.22.D7B39 2001   917.9504'1   C2001-910240-2

Project coordination and graphics by Paul Marcano
Printed and bound in Canada by Friesen Printers
Printed on acid-free paper

The publisher gratefully acknowledges the kind assistance rendered by Douglas and McIntyre Ltd. and by Friesen Printers to enable publication of this book.

Contents

vi

Maps and Illustrations

Tables

Acknowledgements

This book is the product of a research project which could not have been undertaken and completed without the support, advice and encouragement of many people. To begin, credit is due to Bob Ward for rekindling my interest in the possibility that Europeans reached British Columbia's shores long before the first explorers of record. I wish to thank him for supplying me in the first instance with copies of some of the scholarly literature, including his own publications on the subject, and for sharing with me his subsequent discovery of the altered latitude in the manuscript known as the *Anonymous Narrative*.

There was an essential need to develop a new investigative framework around the question of Drake's whereabouts, and sincere thanks are due to Dr. Tim Ball for the many hours which he spent discussing this with me; also for tutoring me in the climate of the Little Ice Age, and for many other kindnesses. Although the subject predates the previously accepted history of Europeans on this coast by two centuries, the British Columbia Archives has a fine library of material relating to European maritime development and exploration in the 16th century. My thanks to all of the staff of that fine institution. As my need to examine the contemporary maps and documents grew, I found the institutions where they are preserved were without exception most helpful. Special thanks are due to Francis Herbert of the Royal Geographical Society; to Peter Barber and Geoff Armitage of the Map Library, and Dr. Michelle Brown of the Department of Manuscripts, The British Library; and to Alan Jutzi in Rare Books, the Huntington Library for their many efforts to assist me. Thank you also to Anthony Payne of Bernard Quaritch Ltd. for the hours spent examining the *Anonymous Narrative* with me.

The initial draft of my research manuscript was voluminous. Nevertheless several very knowledgeable people kindly took the trouble to plough through it and offer many useful comments. These were:

Dr. Timothy F. Ball, geographer, British Columbia
Walter Hardwick, Emeritus Professor, geography, University
    of British Columbia
Francis Herbert, Curator of Maps, Royal Geographical Society, London
Grant Keddie, Curator of Archaeology, Royal British Columbia Museum
Dr. George MacDonald, President, Canadian Museum of Civilization
Dr. Robert McGhee, archaeologist, Canadian Museum of Civilization

David B. Quinn, Emeritus Professor, history, University of Liverpool
Richard I. Ruggles, Emeritus Professor, geography, Queens University, Kingston

My thanks to all, and particularly to Professor Quinn who took the trouble to write a thoughtful and encouraging response. Sincere thanks also to the five reviewers who wrote to the Government of British Columbia stating their support for my principal conclusion. I am especially indebted to Professor Ruggles who spent many hours sharing his knowledge of the cartography of discovery, and offering steady encouragement for my investigations. The following persons then kindly joined the review of my work in its second draft:

Dr. Marcel van den Broecke, historian of the works of Ortelius, Netherlands
Dr. Andrew S. Cook, historian of hydrographic survey, London
Jonathan C.H. King, Curator of Ethnography for North America, The British Museum
Rodney Shirley, historian of cartography, London
Thomas H.B. Symons, Vanier Professor Emeritus, history, Trent University and Chairman of the Frobisher archival research group
Jim Thomson, historical archaeologist, U.S. National Park Service
Norman J.W. Thrower, Emeritus Professor, geography, University of California at Los Angeles
Dr. Stephanie Toothman, historian, U.S. National Park Service
Professor Glyndwr Williams, historian, Queen Mary and Westfield College, University of London
Professor Robin Winks, historian, Yale University

I thank all for taking the time to review this work and to offer their comments and suggestions. It should not, however, be inferred from these acknowledgements that any of the persons named is responsible in any way for the contents of this book. I am the sole person responsible for its contents and conclusions.

And lastly, I would like to thank Dianne Fidler for the countless hours which she has devoted to transcribing my handwritten manuscript into this attractive document.

x

An Enduring Mystery

And the 26. of Sept [1580] ... we safely with ioyful minds and thankful hearts to God, arriued at Plimoth, the place of our first setting forth after we had spent 2. years 10. moneths, and some few odde dais beside, in seeing the wonders of the Lord in the deep, in discouering so many admirable things, in going through with so many strange aduentures, in escaping out of so many dangers, and ouercoming so many difficulties in this our encompassing of this neather globe, and passing round the world

With these words the narrator of *The World Encompassed by Sir Francis Drake* concludes his account of one of the most celebrated voyages in history.[1] Francis Drake, scourge of the Spanish Main, was back at last, his *Golden Hinde* carrying a huge haul of treasure. This time he had sailed through Magellan's Strait, plundered Spanish shipping on the coasts of Chile, Peru and New Spain, and then continued right around the world. Drake's mission had been shrouded in secrecy from the outset, the story having been given out when he departed that he was bound for Alexandria on a trading expedition. Then in August 1579 word of his raids had reached Seville, where nervous English merchants relayed it to London. But the last the Spanish colonials had seen of Drake was at the little Central American port of Guatulco in April of that year, after which he had vanished. Seventeen months had passed since then, and his backers had begun to fear that he would never be seen again. Now he lay at anchor behind an island outside the main harbour of Plymouth while his trumpeter rode to London to inform Sir Christopher Hatton, captain of Queen Elizabeth's bodyguard, of his return.

Within a week a message arrived from the Queen summoning Drake. By the time he reached London, the city was already buzzing with rumours of his extraordinary adventure. But then a veil of secrecy descended. Notwithstanding that Drake had performed the greatest voyage in his nation's history and would subsequently be knighted for the feat, publication of any details of his adventure was strictly prohibited. Drake went on to further fame as a naval commander in the war with Spain, and books, pictures and ballads were published in his praise, but for nearly a decade thereafter none contained any geographical particulars of his great voyage.[2]

At last in 1589 Richard Hakluyt, the leading propagandist for English overseas enterprise, wrote in the title page to his forthcoming collection of voyages that it would include an account of an expedition to the South Sea and "*Nova Albion* vpon the backside of *Canada*, further than any Christian hitherto hath pierced".[3] Albion was an ancient name for Britain, so Hakluyt was in effect announcing that the *New England* was located on the Pacific coast of the northern region the French called Canada. When Hakluyt's book appeared in print, however, it did not include this promised story, and when the account, titled "The Famous Voyage", was finally released some time later [4], the location given for Nova Albion had been changed. Hakluyt now wrote that after taking a "somewhat northerly" course to latitude 42 degrees, Drake turned back and found a harbour at 38 degrees (near present San Francisco), where he careened the *Golden Hinde* for repairs before resuming his voyage across the Pacific. Because of the friendly reception by the Indians at this anchorage, Hakluyt said, Drake took possession of the surrounding country for Elizabeth and named it Nova Albion. Then, following the release of this account, Hakluyt made further changes to the basic information in his second edition.[5] This problem of inconsistency is not confined to Hakluyt's accounts however. There are several contemporary accounts and maps of Drake's voyage, and every one of them presents information which is in some way significantly different from the others regarding the extent of Drake's voyage into the North Pacific. Consequently there has been much controversy surrounding the question of his actual whereabouts in the region.

When the California gold rush brought the city of San Francisco to life, its citizens eagerly embraced the story that Drake had landed somewhere nearby, and began looking for the harbour where his men had set up a fortified camp and spent five weeks repairing the *Golden Hinde*. Some opined that Drake had anchored in the very Bay of San Francisco, while others favoured one of the bays a short distance to the north: Bodega Bay, or the bay that the Spanish had named Drake's Bay when they settled in the area at the end of the 18th century.[6] In 1890 however, the California Historical Society published a paper by Professor George Davidson, a member of the U.S. Coast and Geodetic Survey, pronouncing that Drake's Bay was the true site of Drake's careenage. Although at odds with the experiences and observations of several early explorers of the coast, Davidson's opinion was widely accepted.[7]

Then in 1914 the Hakluyt Society, dedicated to the study of maritime history, published a volume of research by Zelia Nuttall titled *New Light on Drake*. Searching in New and Old World archives, Miss Nuttall had found and translated a wealth of new information in hitherto unnoticed Spanish documents. These were the depositions of various captives taken and later released by Drake, as well as testimony given to the Inquisition by several Englishmen captured by the Spanish before and after Drake's voyage. Integrating this information with that from English sources, Nuttall argued that Drake's mission had been defined by Queen Elizabeth herself, and that one of his objectives was to discover the Pacific entrance to the Northwest Passage. Also, referring to the testimony of several of Drake's countrymen, Nuttall concluded that it had been Drake's "dream" to establish a colony at Nova Albion.[8] And regarding the extent of his northern voyage, she presented a little known map which depicts Drake's track continuing north in the Pacific to an inscription, "turned back because of the ice", inferring that Drake had gone much further north than previously supposed.[9]

In 1926 California historian Henry R. Wagner published a major work on the aims and achievements of Drake's voyage in which he took strong exception to Nuttall's arguments.[10] Any notion that Drake was interested in exploration or colonization, Wagner said, was preposterous. Nuttall's suggestions that Drake had in mind a larger purpose than finding a harbour in which to repair his ship when he sailed north from Central America, that he was acting on Elizabeth's instructions, and that he might have gone much further north were, he said, completely without foundation, as was any idea that he envisioned establishing a colony at Nova Albion.[11] Drake may have careened his ship further north than previously thought, Wagner said, but certainly not beyond northern California. The locus of Drake's exploit, he insisted, was California, and there was no evidence of any value to support any other conclusion.

In the 1930's however, a new perspective began to emerge from the work of historical geographer E.G.R. Taylor.[12] Examining the writings of the men who had shaped English geographical thought prior to Drake's voyage, she showed that their vision was focused on reaching the as yet undiscovered lands on the far side of the globe where ancient writings and the stories of travellers such as Marco Polo told of immense riches to be had, and that central to this vision was the aim of discovering a searoute either to the northeast around Asia, or to the northwest around America into the South Sea. Then in 1939 Wagner's view of Drake's northern voyage was challenged by R.P. Bishop, a former Royal Navy officer who had extensive knowledge of sailing in the North Pacific in square-rigged ships.[13] Comparing Hakluyt's description of Drake's course northward from Central America with the information provided by other sources, Bishop found the latter more believable because they reflected what Drake would have learned from his interrogation of the several Spanish pilots whom he captured. Reconstructing Drake's course from those sources, Bishop showed that he had sailed in a great arc following the circulation of winds in the North Pacific, and that this would have brought him onto the northwest coast of America well north of California, in the vicinity of Vancouver Island.

These analyses received little notice in California, however, because in 1937 a brass plate which appeared to be inscribed with Drake's proclamation of Nova Albion was brought to the University of California at Berkeley. After examining the plate, the director of the Bancroft Library pronounced it to be authentic.[14] But it purportedly had been found some distance inland (in Marin County, north of San Francisco), and so the question of where Drake had landed was still unresolved. After World War II, several groups argued in support of the various contending bays and the anchorage debate intensified.[15] The problem was, as the years passed no hard evidence was found which connected Drake with any of these bays. None of them closely resembles the drawing of the anchorage which appears in the corner of a contemporary map depicting his voyage, and efforts to find the remnants of the fortified camp where Drake spent five weeks proved fruitless. Then, with the quadricentennary of the voyage approaching, the plate of brass was sent to several laboratories for metallurgical tests. The conclusion from these tests was that the brass was of modern manufacture—the plate was a hoax.[16]

Then in 1984 the University of California published a volume of essays on Drake's voyage edited by Professor Norman J.W. Thrower, former chairman of the Sir Francis Drake Commission of the State of California. In one essay Professor David B. Quinn, a leading authority on the writings of Richard Hakluyt, laid out a compelling argument that Hakluyt's account of the voyage into the North Pacific was adapted from a draft of *The World Encompassed by Sir Francis Drake*, which had been written under Drake's personal supervision but then suppressed and not finally published until 1628, many years after his death.[17] In another essay, noted map historian Helen Wallis documented the imposition of official secrecy around Drake's voyage and argued that this led to the many contradictory claims in its aftermath and deprived Drake of credit for his discoveries.[18]

Meanwhile another anchorage sleuth, Bob Ward, published the first in a series of articles contending that he has found Drake's careenage on the coast of Oregon.[19] Finding in a contemporary manuscript account of Drake's voyage that it placed this bay at latitude 44°, Ward had examined the coastline in that vicinity and discovered that Whale Cove closely matches the contemporary drawing of Drake's careenage. On further investigation he learned that a number of metal artifacts predating the 18th century explorers, including an Elizabethan coin, had been found along the coast from Whale Cove northward to Cape Flattery. Ward theorized that Drake sailed into the Strait of Juan de Fuca and then, concluding that he had discovered the Pacific entrance to the northwest passage, returned southward, repaired his ship at Whale Cove and gave the name Nova Albion to the surrounding country (Oregon). Ward has contributed several valuable new pieces of evidence concerning Drake's northern voyage, and his argument for Whale Cove as the site of Drake's careenage deserves serious consideration. However, it does not explain the widely varying accounts and maps of the voyage in the contemporary record, many of which suggest that Nova Albion and Drake's careenage were separate places. And the one point on which the sources are in agreement is that the bay where Drake stopped to repair the *Golden Hinde* was virtually the last and southernmost point he reached on the coast of North America, after a more northerly voyage. Therefore, finding the socalled "lost harbour" where Drake repaired his ship will not, by itself, answer the most intriguing questions, which are: how far north *did* he go and what *did* he discover?

To find the answers to these questions it is necessary to begin afresh and re-examine the record of Drake's voyage without any preconception regarding the location of his eventual careenage. His discovery and use of this harbour was preceded by, and resulted from a singular progression of events about which there were many conflicting representations in the aftermath of the voyage. This is the crux of the mystery surrounding Drake's northern exploit. So were these representations merely speculations based on rumour, or were they produced by persons who had a connection to Drake and thereby possessed or were given specific information concerning the voyage? If the latter, then clearly most or all of the variations were deliberate deviations from the truth. It follows, then, that if all of the variations could be satisfactorily explained, that explanation should reveal the true scope of the voyage.

To this end, there is need for an improved understanding of the genesis of the contemporary accounts and maps. This is not to suggest that there has not already been much good work on the subject. Indeed, the present contribution would have been impossible but for a host of valuable efforts by others, as will be seen. However, the written and cartographic records have tended to be treated as separate fields of inquiry, which has resulted in only partial integration of the information. There is therefore an opportunity to develop a stronger synthesis, particularly by integrating the chronologies of the material. It then becomes possible to trace the evolution of the information over time and to identify the persons behind its production and dissemination. Examination of one of the documents reveals that the information has been enciphered. Then comparison of the details in the maps with the actual coastline enables the information to be deciphered and the rules of encipherment to be exposed. This in turn leads to the discovery of other details provided in maps not previously associated with Drake's voyage. Combining all of the information, a surprisingly coherent picture emerges and it becomes possible to reconstruct Drake's movements in the North Pacific with remarkable clarity, and to appreciate fully the implications of his discoveries and the reasons his northern voyage was so tightly wrapped in secrecy.

6

CHAPTER ONE

A Strategically Vital Quest

Francis Drake's voyage to the South Sea was the culmination of a vision whose roots ran well back in time, and it is essential to begin with an appreciation of this background. It will be remembered that for many years previous in England some men had held a passionate interest in the possibility of reaching the East Indies, where Portuguese explorations via the Cape of Good Hope had opened up a fabulous trade in spices, silk and other precious commodities. To this, Ferdinand Magellan's discovery in 1520 that the South Sea was a vast ocean had added the realization that there may be other, as yet undiscovered lands to the north and south of his route which contained great riches. However, Spain and Portugal had entered into the Treaty of Tordesillas under which they had divided the rights to occupy and exploit all non-Christian lands between themselves exclusively, and any attempt to penetrate southward into either of their spheres would mean fighting.

The quest for a northern route into the South Sea originated in the voyage of John Cabot's son Sebastian. In 1508 the younger Cabot followed the coast of the Newfound Land northward until he encountered great icebergs and there was almost continuous daylight. Sebastian Cabot believed that the passage could be discovered, but finding little support in England for further voyages he went into the service of Spain, eventually rising to the position of Pilot Major overseeing the development of Spanish navigation. Through the reign of King Henry VIII, discovery of a northern passage was advocated by Robert Thorne, Roger Barlow and others, but Henry showed little interest in exploration. Following Henry's death in 1547 however, Sebastian Cabot was persuaded to return to England to head up a new effort in exploration. Cabot proposed to resume the search for a passage to the northwest, around America, but his patrons favoured exploring for a passage to the northeast, around Asia. Finally in 1551 a syndicate of merchants, later known as the Muscovy Company, was granted a monopoly to discover and exploit a northern passage, but its efforts to find a route to the northeast met with failure, and when Cabot died in 1557 the possibility of a further search remained unresolved.[1]

The following year Elizabeth ascended the throne, but through the first decade of her reign the main focus of English overseas enterprise was the efforts of Drake's kinsmen, the Hawkins brothers, to develop trade with Spain's Caribbean colonies. In 1568 however, a sudden Spanish attack destroyed a Hawkins trading expedition at Vera Cruz, Mexico, ending all hope on that front. Drake then embarked on a private war of reprisal against King Philip of Spain, raiding his shipments of Peruvian treasure, which were carried by packtrain across the Isthmus of Panama to

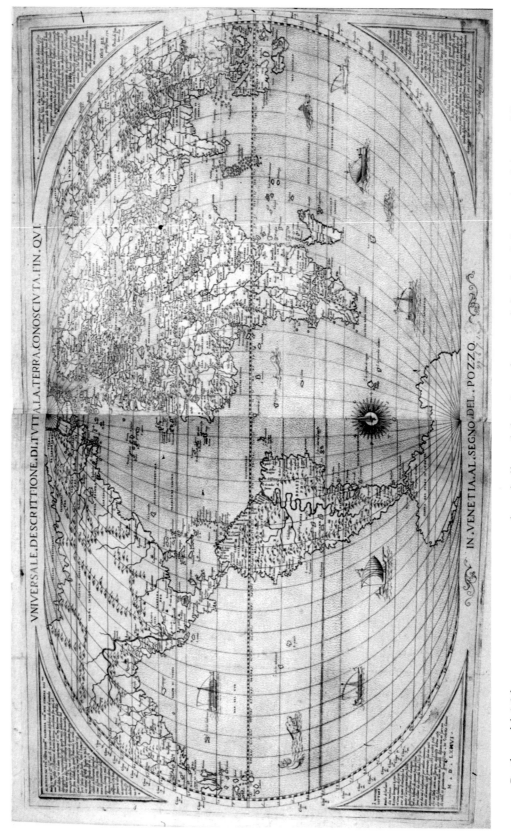

In the mid 16th century many cosmographers believed that America was joined to Asia north of the Pacific Ocean.

By Permission of The British Library

the Caribbean port of Nombre de Dios. On one of his raids Drake trekked across the Isthmus, and viewing the Pacific for the first time, vowed that he would one day sail on that sea. After seizing a shipment of gold he returned to England in 1573 determined to pursue his project for a voyage to the South Sea.

In the meantime the Spanish had continued exploring the South Sea. After the voyage of Loaysa, they had abandoned Magellan's hazardous route through the strait which he had found at the extremity of South America and thereafter further explorations were launched from the Pacific coast of America. Initially their focus had been the development of navigation southward from Panama to support their conquest and exploitation of Peru. Then they turned their attention to finding a viable return route from Magellan's Philippine Islands back across the Pacific to New Spain, but the solution eluded them for many years. Finally in 1565 Friar Urdaneta solved the problem by sailing north from the Philippines until he picked up the westerlies between latitudes 35° and 40° N, which brought him back onto the coast of *the Californias*. However, no Spaniard had ventured much beyond latitude 40° in the North Pacific, and the possibility of rivals intruding into his ocean via a northern passage from Europe was a growing concern to King Philip. Urdaneta believed a passage existed and advised Philip that its Pacific entrance should be located and fortified against foreign use, but development of the trans-Pacific trade absorbed the available resources and his recommendation was not acted upon.[2]

At the heart of the possibility of a northern passage, then, lay a fundamental question: was America joined to Asia somewhere north of latitude 40°, or was it a separate continent? If they were joined, there would be no possibility of entering the South Sea via a northern route. In part because the Spanish kept secret their calculations of the sailing distance across the South Sea, lest it be revealed that they were encroaching on Portuguese territory in the Philippines, many cosmographers continued to believe that America was an extension of Asia. In 1564, however, Flemish cartographer Abraham Ortelius produced a map, after that of Gastaldi (1561), which showed them as separate continents divided by a supposed *Strait of Anian*. Ortelius depicted the strait beginning at about latitude 40° in the North Pacific and running northward to a junction with a broad passage reaching westward above America from the Atlantic. And on the Pacific coast of North America, at about latitude 45° he placed *Sierra Nevada*, suggesting a range of snowcapped mountains in that vicinity.

In 1566, soldier-adventurer Sir Humphrey Gilbert began circulating among prominent men in England a crude copy of Ortelius' map, together with a treatise advocating a project to find this northwest passage.[3] Its discovery, he argued, would provide direct access to the richest region of the globe, thus eliminating Spanish and

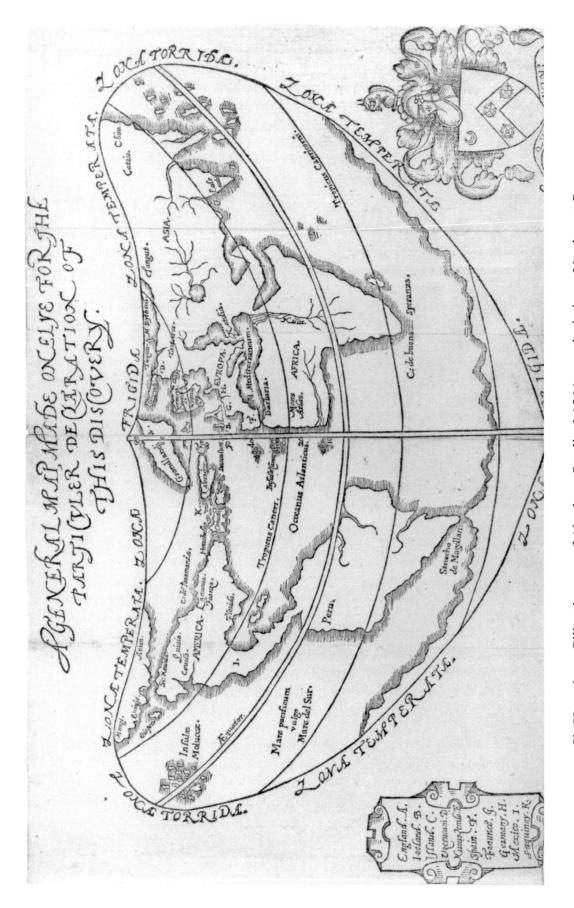

Sir Humphrey Gilbert's copy of Abraham Ortelius' 1564 map depicting a Northwest Passage

By Permission of The British Library

Portuguese middlemen, and would occasion the building of a great navy which would make England the ascendant nation of the world. And to facilitate this result, he wrote, it would be desirable to inhabit "for our staple some place of America, about Sierra Nevada", that is, beyond the snowcapped mountains which Ortelius postulated on his map. Here then is the first concept of an English colony on the northwest coast of America, as an essential adjunct to discovery of the northwest passage, to serve as a haven where ships emerging from the Strait of Anian would stop to repair and reprovision.

Gilbert presented a detailed plan of his project to the Queen, but it got no further due to obstruction by the Muscovy Company. In 1573 however, the complexion of Elizabeth's Privy Council changed significantly with her appointment of Francis Walsingham as secretary of state responsible for foreign affairs and, parenthetically, for espionage and protection of state secrets. Walsingham had already set up at his own expense a network of agents reporting on activity at foreign courts, and was closely allied with the Queen's childhood friend Robert Dudley, now the Earl of Leicester. The two most aggressive personalities in the Privy Council, Walsingham and Leicester were keenly interested in development of overseas enterprise and hereafter would play a leading role in the planning of such ventures. Pressure was brought to bear on the Muscovy Company and early in 1575 they granted a license to their London agent, Michael Lok, and onetime pirate Martin Frobisher to explore for a northwest passage.[4] Organization of the venture dragged however, and soon afterward the Privy Council received another proposal.

The previous year Gilbert's cousin Richard Grenville had sought a license to explore and found colonies in the river Plate and through Magellan's Strait on the Pacific coast of America, to the south of Spain's possessions. Initially Grenville's proposal, made on behalf of a West Country syndicate which included Drake's cousin John Hawkins, had been approved, but then Elizabeth had suddenly ordered a halt to the project. It appears that her senior minister, the ever cautious Lord Burghley, had convinced her that it was bound to provoke a confrontation with Spain. Now however, Grenville submitted a revised proposal. Lok and Frobisher, he wrote, were looking for the northwest passage from the wrong end, that is, from the Atlantic side where its entrance was believed to lie in the ice-filled waters of the arctic. It would be far better, he suggested, to explore for the passage from its western end, via the salubrious climes of the South Sea, where

> besides countries of moste excellente temperature to be inhabited, if we think it necessary, and if we aryve to tymely [too early in the year] to enter the said straighte of Anian, yet have we Cathaia, and all the oriental Indies open vnto us for trafique.[5]

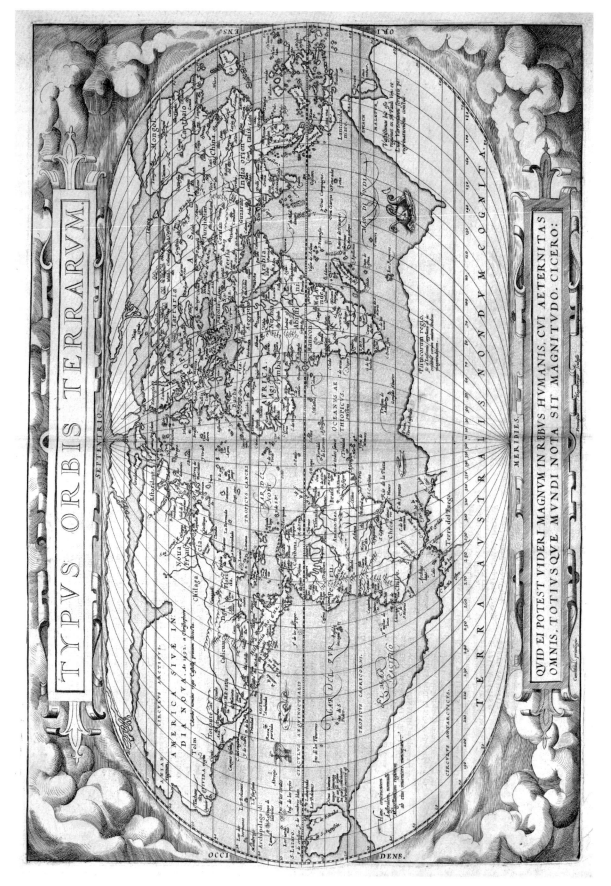

Abraham Ortelius' 1570 world map depicts the Strait of Anian as beginning at latitude 60° in the Pacific and running northward to converge with both Northeast and Northwest Passages at latitude 66°N

By Permission of The British Library

Thus, Grenville argued, even if the Strait of Anian were not found there would still be ample opportunity to obtain a rich cargo before returning home. He proposed a fifteen month voyage; including three months to reach Magellan's Strait, three months to sail from there to latitude 50° in the North Pacific, and three months to explore and map the entrance to the northern strait. Then, after spending three months locating and trading with Cathay he would set sail for home in June, by which season he supposed the passage would be free of ice. Here then is the first mention of an English scheme to discover the northwest passage via Magellan's Strait and the South Sea. However, Grenville did not receive the requisite license to undertake the voyage.

A key figure in the background at this time was the leading English cosmographer, Dr. John Dee.[6] A brilliant mathematician, Dee had studied at the University of Louvain, a centre for geographic and navigational research, and was at the forefront of these fields. One of his mentors at Louvain, Gemma Frisius, had been an advocate for discovery of a northern passage, and after he returned to England Dee had become a member of Sebastian Cabot's circle. Also he had instructed Robert Dudley in geometry and cosmography, and through that connection chiefly had become Elizabeth's astrologer. Now working from his extensive library at Mortlake, near London, Dee corresponded with and collected the works of many of the leading scholars in Europe, and was consulted by some of the most powerful men in England regarding the principal geographical questions of the day.

In March 1576, Dee was visited by Abraham Ortelius, who had come to England to escape the looming Spanish atrocities in his native city of Antwerp. No doubt they had a long discussion about the unexplored regions of the globe, and very likely they consulted Ortelius' latest map of the world, *Typus Orbis Terrarum*. This Ortelius had published with his first atlas in 1570 and was based largely on the work of his colleague, the famous geographer Gerard Mercator, who theorized that there was a great westward bulge in North America which filled much of the unexplored region of the North Pacific. Ortelius' map incorporated this feature and with it Mercator's concept of the Strait of Anian beginning at about latitude 60° and running northward to connect to both northeast and northwest passages at 66°.

Then in May Dee was summoned to Muscovy House, where he spent several days instructing Frobisher and his pilot Christopher Hall in the science of mathematical navigation.[7] Frobisher sailed at the beginning of June and a month later they reached the coast of Greenland, where they were overawed by the huge icebergs drifting along the coast. Continuing west and then northward, Frobisher found between headlands a broad, westward-leading opening which he took to be the hoped-for passage. In reality he had sailed across the entrance to Hudson Strait into the mouth of a large inlet in Baffin Island. After some encounters with the native Inuit people and the disappearance of five of his men, Frobisher collected samples of some unusually heavy rock and then set sail for home to report his discovery.

Soon after Frobisher's return it was announced that the Queen would invest in the project, and then the Privy Council became involved in the planning for a followup voyage.[8] Strangely however, the focus of the venture now changed. Notwithstanding that Frobisher had reported finding the all-important passage, the declared object of the new expedition became collection of more of the heavy rock which he had found, which according to preliminary assays contained gold. Frobisher sailed again in May 1577, returning at the end of summer with more of the supposed ore, and then the following spring he was sent out with 15 ships and returned with some 1500 tonnes of the rock. In all events, it proved worthless. But while the mining enterprise was the immediate commercial object of the voyage, there were other aims as well, and these and the geographical details of Frobisher's discoveries were closely guarded. He was ordered to turn all logs and charts of the voyage over to the government immediately upon his return. In 1577 an account of his second voyage by one Dionese Settle appeared in print, but all this said about the location of his discoveries was:

> I Could declare vnto the Readers the *latitude and longitude* of such places and regions as we have bene at, but not altogether so perfectly as our masters and many other...[therefore] I let them [these particulars] passe to their reports as men most apt to set forth and declare the same.[9]   *(my italics)*

King Philip had heard about the voyages however, and when his new ambassador, Bernardino de Mendoza, arrived in London in March 1578 he had instructions to find out all he could about them.[10] Mendoza immediately set to work expanding Philip's network of spies, and by June he had obtained a chart of the second voyage and reported on preparations for the third. Then, after Frobisher's return that fall Mendoza sent Philip an enciphered report on the third voyage. No one, he said, dared write anything about the voyages as they were "under threat of pain of death" if they did so; but he was able to provide the details because he had a spy who had accompanied Frobisher.[11] Notably, Frobisher's orders had included building a fort which would be manned by 100 men with provisions for 18 months. Then, once construction and mining were underway he was to explore 50 to 100 leagues further into his strait, and to record the time of summer when it was most free of ice. Mendoza's spy told him about the plan to leave men behind, which had to be aborted, and accurately described the events of the voyage.[12]

Allowing that Mendoza's intelligence of Frobisher's voyages was factual, there is no reason to doubt that the threat of "pain of death" to anyone who wrote about them was as well. Discovery of a northern passage was of considerable strategic importance to England, and such an injunction would simply be following the example set by the Spanish, who maintained tight security around the details of their latest discoveries. It therefore appears that Settle's account must have been published for an official purpose, namely to announce England's claim to the region, thereafter called *Meta Incognita*, as made clear by his statement that they "marched through the Countrey with Ensigne displayed ... and now and then heaped up stones on high mountains, and other places in token of possession".[13] Then in late 1578 an account of all three voyages was printed by Henry Binnyman, "servant to the right Honourable Christopher Hatton", and it appears that this account, by Frobisher's lieutenant George Best, was also published under official supervision.[14] It includes a note, "The Printer to the Reader", in which Binnyman explains:

> I have in a fewe places somewhat altered from my copie, and wronged thereby the authoure, *and have sought to conceale upon good causes some secrets not fitte to be published or revealed to the world (as the degrees of longitude and latitude, the distance, and true position of places, and the variation of the compasse)* and which nevertheless, by a generall and [a] particular mappe concerning the same, hereto annexed, is so sufficiently explained ... [as] may sensibly be understode.[15]   (my italics)

Then in his introduction Best explains that one of the maps which he includes has been drawn only "so farre forth as the secrets of the voyage may permit";[16] and indeed, neither of his maps indicates the location of Frobisher's discoveries except in a crudely abstract fashion. Yet both Settle and Binnyman admit that their coordinates had been established. Thus, the production of maps containing deliberately vague or falsified information was an integral part of the official secrecy surrounding the location of Frobisher's strategically vital passage. Ultimately this effort in disinformation proved so effective that after the principal actors died, the location of Meta Incognita became a forgotten secret until 1861 when Charles Francis Hall, while searching for the lost Franklin expedition, was led by the Inuit to the debris of Frobisher's landing on Baffin Island.[17]

But most interesting of all, it appears that in the fall of 1576, despite Frobisher's report that he had found the all-important passage, a decision was taken that he would not attempt to sail to its end, and Best's map of the world does speak to the reason for this. In the map, Frobisher's supposed straits reach far across the top of America until they are connected to the South Sea by a narrow Strait of Anian. The question is obvious: what would Frobisher do if he sailed all that way only to find that this strait did not exist, that America

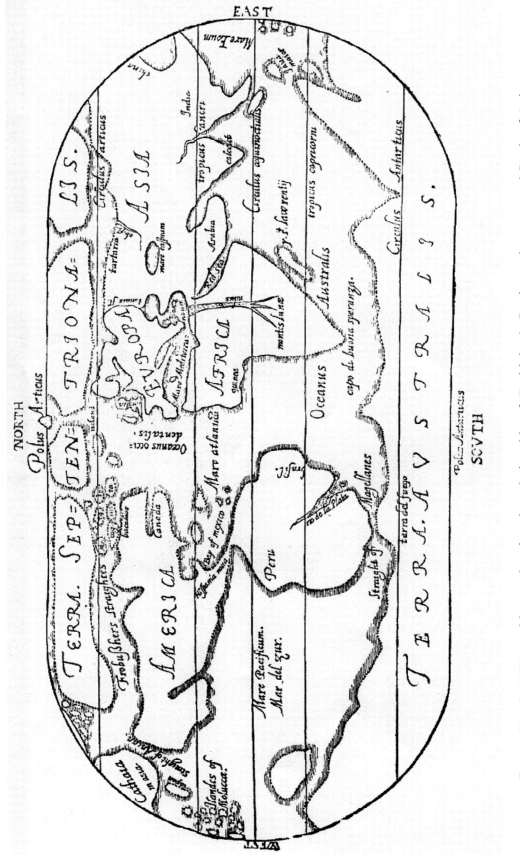

George Best's 1578 world map showing the relationship of Frobisher's Straits to the supposed Strait of Anian

By Permission of The British Library

was in fact joined to Asia as many still believed. It would be too late to sail back before the arctic winter gripped them, and so very likely they would perish. However, he was instructed to probe somewhat further and to report the time when his strait was most clear of ice, and so it appears that by the spring of 1577 other plans were afoot to further the discovery of the northwest passage.

Historian E.G.R. Taylor has pointed to the writings at this juncture of Dr. John Dee.[18] In early August 1576, Dee began writing the first in what would eventually become a series of four volumes on the potential for a British Empire. Notably, the first volume, titled *General and Rare Memorials Pertayning to the Perfect Arte of Navigation*, is dedicated to Christopher Hatton, and Dee explains that his good friend Edward Dyer serves as a constant link between himself and Hatton. Remarkably, Dee completed the manuscript in just six days.[19] In this he writes that it would be advisable if funds were made available for the teaching of a number of foreign languages,

> For that (within these next few years following) with men of all these Cuntries, and farder, Great Affayres are by some of our Cuntrymen to be handled: if God continue his Gracious Direction and Ayde thereto, as he hath very comfortably begonne; and that, by means not yet published.[20]

At first glance it appears that Dee's reference to distant lands and great affairs 'very comfortably begun' but 'not yet published' relates to Frobisher's first voyage in search of the northern passage. But Frobisher had departed two months previous and clearly Dee was newly inspired to have dashed off a volume in just a few days. Moreover, when Frobisher returned that fall with his exciting report, Dee did not add even a veiled reference to it in his work, yet the book was not finally printed until August 1577. Therefore, the timing of his sudden burst of enthusiasm and his allusion to the beginning of an important and evidently confidential project is at least curious.

Dee's second volume, *Queen Elizabeth her Arithmatic Tables Gubernatick: for Navigation by the paradoxall Compass and Navigation in Great Circles*, was completed in the fall of 1576, but has not survived. From the title however, it appears that he was addressing the navigational science required for a long voyage. Even less is known about Dee's third volume other than it was destroyed shortly after completion, possibly, it has been suggested, because it was politically dangerous; that is, contained something which would be vexatious to King Philip.[21] As he continued to write, Dee found time to receive visitors. His diary records that he met on January 16 with the Earl of Leicester and Hatton's man Dyer, and on January 22 with the Earl of Bedford, Francis Drake's godfather.[22] Then on 30 March 1577 Dee commenced writing his fourth volume, titled *The Great Volume of*

Rich and Famous Discoveries. In this he recounts the legends of fabulous wealth in the South Sea and endeavours to locate the places where it is to be found, referring to Ortelius' interpretation of the region. Next he turns to the challenge of discovering the Strait of Anian, citing Spanish attempts to do so by land and by sea. Then he writes:

> Of how great Importance then imagine you is that Attempt which is by a British Subiect presently intended...who (God sparing life & health) hath resolutely offred ... the employing of all his skill and talent, & the patient enduring of the great toyle of his body to that plac being the very end of the world from us to be reckoned to accomplish that Discovery wch of so many & so valiant captayns by land & by sea hath byn so oft attempted in vain.[23]

In the adjacent margin, Dee notes "A worthy attempt at Discovery, faithfully intended by a true Brytish Subiect". Dee wrote this on 15 May 1577, and the following week Frobisher would embark on his second voyage, but this could hardly be characterized as an expedition to 'the very end of the world from us to be reckoned'. Moreover, as has been seen the primary purpose of his voyage was to collect more of his supposed ore. Clearly Dee's reference to captains attempting to 'accomplish that discovery' by land and sea relates to the Spanish efforts to find the Strait of Anian which he cites in his preceding text. Here then was the basis for his sudden burst of enthusiasm in August of 1576 about 'great affairs' and the need to learn several foreign languages.[24] Certainly Dee would not have considered any plan to discover a northern passage 'comfortably begun' without a commitment to solve the question of the Strait of Anian. And clearly the only practical means of doing so would be to send an expedition to the South Sea and northward to the 'very end of the world from us', as reckoned in sailing distance, just as Grenville had proposed.

A key to understanding what was going on behind the scenes through this period is the construction of Drake's flagship *Pelican*, later renamed the *Golden Hinde*. Notably, her hull was specially double-planked. It has been suggested that this was to withstand the ravages of the *toredo worm*, but there may be a better explanation. In any case, allowing that she was to sail for the South Sea, she certainly would not have been built in haste. A reasonable allowance of time for her construction and fitting out would be at least five or six months. And it is reasonable to think that her building was undertaken after Drake received the go-ahead for his proposed voyage and had an opportunity to consider the features which should be incorporated in her design. Then there would be the problem of keeping his plans from Mendoza's spies in Plymouth and at Elizabeth's court. Thus, we find Drake's kinsman John Hawkins writing in June 1577 for Walsingham to circulate, a fictitious plan in which Drake is to command the *Pelican* and a second ship, the *Swallow*, on a voyage to

Alexandria.[25]   Mention of the *Pelican* at this juncture establishes that she had already been christened, and indeed on 9 July 1577 Drake claimed the royal bounty on her completed construction.[26]   It therefore appears that he must have begun considering her design sometime in the fall of 1576.

To this picture we may now add some undated and partially burnt memoranda, apparently prepared for Walsingham to present the case for Drake's voyage to the Queen.[27]   The first page refers to Drake's ship as the *Francis* and to six pinnaces which are to be carried in her hold.   From identification of Drake's ship as the *Francis* it appears that the idea of building a new ship for the purpose had not yet been considered when these memoranda were written.   The second page lists the participants in the venture and credits Drake with a contribution of £1,000.   Notably, his backers include Leicester, Walsingham, Hatton, Hawkins and the Lord Admiral Lincoln.   Next there is a memorandum in which Walsingham is asked to see whether the Queen will lend the her ship the *Swallow*, and to ensure that she is "mayde pryve to the trewthe of the viage, and yet the cooller [colour, or story] to be given owt [that it would be destined] for allixandria".   Evidently these undated papers predate Elizabeth's consent for the project.

The next item is a draft plan of the voyage, and although it has been partially burnt, it is nevertheless quite apparent that this does not contain the 'truth of the voyage' which Walsingham was to convey to the Queen.   What can be made out looks like nothing more than a repetition of Grenville's original proposal to found colonies at the extremity of South America.   It is patently obvious, however, that Drake was intent on raiding the coasts of Chile and Peru, and he would not have dared to conceal this intention from such powerful associates.   Most probably then, the truth of the voyage was not set down on paper for fear that Philip's spies might get ahold of the document.   But it is conceivable that a search for the Strait of Anian did not form a part of the true plan which Walsingham conveyed to the Queen in the first instance.   It is interesting then, that the last note in these memoranda is a reminder to Walsingham that he should urge the Queen's approval with all possible speed, or the voyage "cannot take the good effect, as it is hoepped for".[28]   It appears that Drake may originally have hoped to sail before the end of 1576.   In all events the voyage was postponed for a year, and the reason appears to be Drake's decision to build a new ship with a strong, double-planked hull.   So was this delay and additional expense incurred in order to withstand the ravages of the *toredo worm*; or was it so that Drake would have an especially sturdy ship with which to endure a voyage among the perilous ice floes which Frobisher reported when he returned that fall from his first voyage?   The suggestion is that it was for the latter reason because shortly before Dee began excitedly writing in August 1576, Drake had committed to search for the Strait of Anian, and if successful, attempt to return that way to England.

The Golden Hinde
Profile of the fine replica, constructed in 1974

Courtesy of Rodney Coleman

CHAPTER TWO

Early Accounts of the Northern Voyage

We turn now to the documents produced in the aftermath of Drake's voyage, beginning with testimony given before the Spanish Inquisition while Drake was still in the Pacific.[1] John Oxenham was Drake's lieutenant in his raid on Nombre de Dios, and then on a subsequent expedition in 1576 he crossed the Isthmus of Panama with 70 men and assembled a small vessel on the Pacific coast, but was captured by the Spanish and imprisoned at Lima. Within days of Drake's raid on Lima's harbour, Callao, in February 1579 Oxenham and two of his men were interrogated in an effort to determine the background to Drake's voyage.[2] To begin, they said, no company of armed ships could possibly have sailed for the New World without the permission of their Queen. Oxenham told of Grenville's project to enter the South Sea and said that he had joined the expedition, but then the Queen had revoked Grenville's license for the voyage. Oxenham said that when he left England Drake was waiting for an opportunity to launch his own expedition, and

> Witness thinks that if the Queen were to give a license to Captain Francis Drake he would certainly come and pass through the Strait because he his a very good mariner and pilot, and there is no better one than he in England who could accomplish this ... The said Captain Francis had often spoken to witness saying that if the Queen would grant him the license he would pass through the Strait of Magellan and found settlements over here in some good country.[3]

Asked how many ships Drake would bring, Oxenham replied that with the aid of his relatives and others he might bring two or three, but that after discovering a "good country" they would be able to return with more. And:

> Questioned whether they had discussed how, and by what route, they were to return to England after having passed through the Strait, he [Oxenham] said that it seemed to him that some said it was to be by the same Strait, but others said that there was a route through another Strait that passed into the North Sea, but nobody knows this for certainty or has passed through it.[4]

Thus, even before Drake had reached the coast of Central America the Spanish had begun to form a disquieting picture of Drake's larger purpose. Then in May 1579 Nuño da Silva, the Portuguese pilot whom Drake had captured in the Cape Verde Islands and finally put ashore fifteen months later at Guatulco, was brought before the Inquisition in Mexico City for interrogation as a suspected Drake collaborator.

Da Silva said Drake told him that he had come for an "other purpose" than the seizing of ships, and that

> in Guatulco Drake took out a map and pointed out on it how he had to return by a strait which is in 66° ... Many times he told me and some Spaniards whom he captured that he had to return by the Strait of the Bacallaos [northwest passage] which he came to discover ... He said that by August, 1579, he had to be back in his own country.[5]

It appears that the map which Drake had shown da Silva was either Mercator's world map or Ortelius' *Typus Orbis Terrarum* derived from it, and especially interesting is da Silva's testimony that Drake was expected to be back in England within a few months.

Meanwhile Captain John Winter, who had lost contact with Drake and turned back after their exit from Magellan's Strait, reached England in the bark *Elizabeth* on 2 June 1579 and immediately submitted a report to the Privy Council.[6] A week later ambassador Mendoza was able to send King Philip a description of Drake's voyage to Magellan's Strait.[7] Then in August reports of Drake's raids began to reach Seville, where English merchants relayed the news to London. Mendoza wrote that Drake's backers included some of Elizabeth's councillors, and that they were overjoyed with the news.[8] Then in December he reported that men were being appointed in each of the ports to assist Drake when he returned.[9] In February 1580 however, Mendoza reported that Drake's backers were beginning to worry that something had happened to him, and were considering sending a ship to search for him.[10] Certainly they could not have expected Drake to return via Magellan's Strait or complete a circumnavigation of the globe in this time. Indeed they had the example of Winter, who had taken nearly eight months just to return from the extremity of South America. Evidently then, da Silva's information was sound. Drake's backers must have been expecting that he would come back via the northwest passage. However, he had not returned at the expected time and many more months passed before he finally arrived at Plymouth on 26 September 1580.

Then on 16 October, three weeks after Drake's return, Mendoza wrote to Philip relating what his spies had learned. Not surprisingly, it is the only account we have of Drake's initial meetings with the Queen and his backers. Indeed it appears that they were anxious to find out what Mendoza knew, as Walsingham's secret service intercepted his dispatch. Mendoza said that Drake had met with Elizabeth for more than six hours and had presented her with "a diary of everything that had happened during the three years and a very large map", but that her councillors "are very particular not to divulge the route by which he returned". He said Drake was proposing to go back to the Pacific immediately with six ships, and was offering a return of seven pounds for every one invested. Drake's men, he said, "are not to disclose the route they took on *pain on death*. Drake affirms, that he will be able to make the round voyage in a year, *as he has found a very short way*"[11] (my italics). Here then was the same injunction previously imposed on Frobisher's men. And in light of all the foregoing, there can be little doubt as to the meaning of the words 'a very short way'. The obvious inference is that Drake had reported that he had found the Strait of Anian, and was now proposing to return with a new expedition to complete the discovery of the northwest passage.

That Drake was proposing a new project is then confirmed by a draft charter for the venture, prepared by Walsingham shortly thereafter. In consideration of his "late notable discovery" Drake was to serve as lifetime governor of the enterprise and receive ten percent of the profits while the Queen was to receive twenty percent.[12] Significantly, Walsingham's proposal evidently upset the Muscovy Company, for on 16 December they presented a counter-petition requesting that the Queen re-affirm their monopoly over exploitation of any northern discovery.[13] It appears that this problem was getting worked out however, because on 15 January Mendoza reported that Drake had not settled accounts with his crew, but instead was keeping them in hand with small sums while attempting to persuade them to go with him on the new expedition.[14] Then later in January he reported that Drake was to take ten ships out via Cape of Good Hope and rendezvous in the Moluccas with Leicester's brother-in-law Francis Knollys, who was to bring six more ships via Magellan's Strait.[15] Clearly this was a major project. But it is impossible to believe that Drake would take such a large force all the way to the South Sea and then leave Philip's treasure shipments untouched, and so it is suggested here that as with his first voyage the true plan had been concealed and 'the Moluccas' was simply a codename for a different scheme.

On 6 April 1581 however, Mendoza reported "it is decided that Drake himself shall not go, although, no doubt, he has arranged the matter through other hands in order that he may not be too conspicuous".[16] Once again Mendoza's intelligence was reliable; Drake would be one of the principal investors, but would not go with the expedition. It appears Elizabeth feared that unleashing him again would provoke a war which would put her throne in serious jeopardy. Still to be resolved however, was the question of who would lead a scaled-down followup expedition to the Pacific, and this was not settled until September when Mendoza reported that Martin Frobisher had been appointed to the command. But the following February as the ships were being prepared the erstwhile pirate Frobisher suddenly resigned and was replaced by his arctic lieutenant Edward Fenton, and it appears that Elizabeth had vetoed all thoughts of plundering Spanish shipping. With this aim stripped from the plan then, it is most interesting to see what purpose there remained in the voyage.

In February 1582 Mendoza reported that the expedition was to include thirty carpenters and thirty bricklayers, leading him to conclude that its aim was to found a colony.[17]   Then on 2 April Fenton's commission was signed by the Queen. According to this the purpose of the voyage was to be "for the discovery of Cathiea & China *as all other lands and ylands allredy discovered* & hereafter to be discovered", and Fenton was authorized to leave behind "*to enhabyte & dwell in and uppon the same land*" as many of his company as he thought advisable[18] (my italics). This was followed on 9 April by the Privy Council's detailed instructions for the voyage. These make no mention of setting up a land base, however, and regarding Fenton's principal objective are strangely incongruous. In the South Sea he was not to pass to the northeastward of latitude 40°—meaning presumably latitude 40° S, that is, to steer clear of Philip's South American possessions—but to take "youre right course to the Iles of the Moluccas for the better discouerie of the Northwest passage, if ... within the same degree of latitude, you can get any knowledge of the passage".[19] What is incongruous is the Moluccas are situated near the Equator in the western Pacific, so the idea of remaining within that latitude certainly would not be conducive to better discovery of the northwest passage. Again then, it appears that 'the Moluccas' was code for another destination which could not be put to paper for fear that Mendoza's spies might get ahold of the document.[20]

Then on 11 April Leicester and Walsingham wrote to Fenton instructing him that Christopher Carleill, who was to accompany the expedition with responsibility for land operations, was to be put in charge of those left behind.[21] The appointment of Carleill, who was Walsingham's stepson, underscores the importance which was placed on this development. It certainly does not appear that this was to be merely the setting up of a careenage or temporary staging area, and obviously its location must have been recommended by Drake and was related to the new venture that he had proposed based on his reported discovery of 'a very short way'. The picture we have then, is that Fenton's voyage was a direct outgrowth of Drake's proposal for a new venture, and leaving aside the question of whether plundering Spanish shipping enroute was to be permitted, the underlying objective of the expedition was to complete the discovery of the northwest passage and set up and inhabit a permanent base of operations—England's first overseas colony—at a secret location somewhere in the Pacific.

While Fenton was receiving his instructions Richard Hakluyt, the aspiring propagandist for English maritime enterprise, was printing his first survey of overseas voyages, titled *Diverse Voyages touching the discouerie of America, and the Ilands adiacent*. In this, Hakluyt lists "Francis Drake Englishman" among the "names of certaine late trauaylers" and alludes to his discoveries "on the back side of America" as encouraging the hope of finding a northwest passage.[22] Included in the

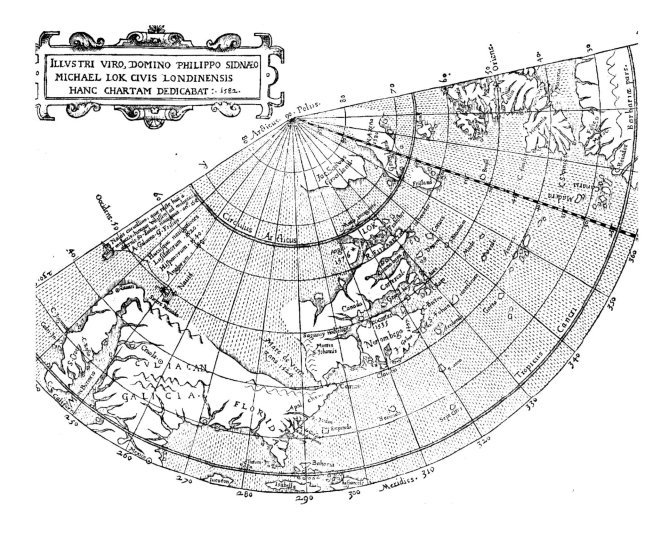

Michael Lok's 1582 map indicating an English reconnaissance
of the Northwest Coast of America

By Permission of The British Library

book is a map by Frobisher's former partner Michael Lok depicting the relationship
of England to his strait and the Pacific coast of America. On the Pacific coast, a ship
is depicted at about latitude 48° beyond a range of mountains labelled *Sierra
Nevada*, and above this is inscribed *Anglorum 1580*. The clear inference then, is that
both ends of the northwest passage had now been reconnoitred. However, these are
the only references to an English voyage in the North Pacific known to have been
published in England prior to 1589.

Fenton finally sailed on 1 May 1582.[23]   Accompanying him were several men who had circumnavigated the globe with Drake, including his trusted lieutenant William Hawkins as Lieutenant-General, pilots Thomas Blacoller and Thomas Hood, and his young cousin John Drake, who was given command of the little *Bark Francis*.   The master of Fenton's flagship *Leicester* was Christopher Hall, who had served as chief pilot on Frobisher's arctic voyages.   Serving as Fenton's chaplain and official recorder was Oxford graduate and lecturer Richard Madox, who subsequently died on the voyage, but who left a diary, much of it in cypher.[24] Evidently Madox was eager to learn more about their destination, as his diary contains some notes obviously derived from conversations with Drake's men.   These include a brief description of the Indians whom Drake had met at a northern landing,

> In ships land wh is ye back side of Labradore and as Mr. Haul supposeth ny thereunto, [where] Syr Francis Drake graved and bremd his ship at 48 degrees to ye north.[25]

This is the earliest known writing of a latitude for Drake in the North Pacific. Equally important is the reference to navigator Hall's belief that the northwest coast of America was not very far from Labrador, meaning presumably not as distant as suggested by the great continental bulge depicted in the map of Ortelius for example. This implies some confidence of its position in longitude, which is all the more interesting because prior to leaving England Madox had written a long entry in his diary about the theory of determining longitude by the lunar distance method.[26]   Dr. Dee undoubtedly was familiar with the theory, and one of his disciples, William Bourne, had described it in his manual on navigation, *A Regiment for the Sea*, first published in 1574.   The theory entailed the use of a book of *Ephemerides*, in which the daily position of the moon would be tabulated so that her distance from a particular star at any hour could be predicted.   Then an observer finding her at a greater or lesser distance from that star and knowing her rate of motion could calculate the difference in time between his position and the meridian where the *Ephemerides* were calculated, every four minutes of time difference representing one degree of longitude.   However, Bourne cautioned, the observer would require the use of a certain unspecified "precise instrument", and this would be rendered useless by the motion of a ship at sea.[27]   Moreover, little was known at this time about the perturbations of the moon and such calculations were bound to incorporate a significant factor of error.   Nevertheless, it is conceivable that the English were attempting to apply the method, and notably Madox carried on the voyage both a book of *Ephemerides* and what he described as "a very perfect instrument".[28]

Fenton's squadron was not long at sea, however, before he and Drake's men began quarrelling.   Prior to leaving England they learned that King Philip had dispatched a fleet (23 galleons with 3,500 men) to fortify the Strait of Magellan against further intrusions into his ocean. Then when Fenton reached the coast of Brazil he was informed that the Spanish fleet was ahead of them. Drake's men were for continuing the voyage, but Fenton decided to turn back. John Drake deserted with the *Bark Francis* and continued southward, but was shipwrecked in the mouth of the River Plate and taken captive by the Indians. After a year of privation he escaped from the Indians and made contact with the Spanish, who took him to Sante Fe in the interior of Argentina. There he was brought before the Inquisition for interrogation on 24 March 1584. Questioned about Drake's northern voyage, he testified:

> He does not know what day they left Aguatulco only that it was in April and they went to seaward. They sailed continually to the northwest and north-northeast. They travelled for all of April and May, until the middle of June. From the said Aguatulco, which is in 15 degrees, they went to 48 degrees. They met with great storms along the way. The whole sky was dark and full of mist. *Along the route they saw five or six islands. Captain Francis gave one of them the name Saint Bartholomew and another one Saint James. These islands were in 46 and 48 degrees. To the land in 48 degrees Captain Francis gave the name New England. They remained there a month and a half, taking on water and wood and repairing the ship.*[29]   (my italics)

This is the earliest known mention of Nova Albion in any written source. Some time later young Drake was taken to Lima, and there on 8, 9 and 10 January 1587 was examined again. In this testimony he provided a few more details of Drake's northern voyage, including:

> They sailed a thousand leagues [3,000 miles] up to the latitude of forty-four degrees, always sailing close to the wind. After this the wind changed and they went to the Californias. They discovered land in forty-eight degrees ... Here they caulked his large ship and left the one they had taken from Nicaragua ... From here they went only with the one ship, taking a course for the Moluccas.[30]

Beside querying again how far north Drake had gone, it appears the Spanish were particularly interested at this juncture to know what became of the little bark that Drake seized in Central America, which John Drake says they abandoned when they departed the northwest coast for the Moluccas. Notably however, this transcript of his Lima testimony makes no mention of the islands previously described, or of Nova Albion; nor do any of his surviving depositions mention the search for the northern passage referred to by Nuño da Silva. Yet the Spanish clearly would have been interested to learn more on these questions. In 1606 however, Spanish historian Antonio de Herrera published an account of Drake's voyage which obviously is based on John Drake's testimony, and in this it appears that he must have had the use of another, now lost transcript which contained some additional information, as he states that Drake

> sailed ... until he reached the latitude of somewhat more than 45° *with the purpose of seeking the strait which has been referred to.* Francis Drake, on this journey, saw five or six *islands of good land.* He called one Saint Bartholomew, one Saint James, *and another which seemed to be the largest and the best, Nova Albion.* Here he remained a month and a half, *repairing the two ships which he had with him.*[31]
> (my italics)

Thus, it appears that John Drake must have been examined further and admitted the search for the passage, and that they had repaired both ships. Here also is corroboration that the concept of New England was directly associated with the search for the strait. And most importantly, we learn that Drake gave this name to 'the largest and best' of five or six islands 'of good land', obviously meaning islands of a size and character suitable for a colony. The problem is, the furthest John Drake says they sailed was latitude 48°, and in reality there are no islands of any consequence from 48° southward until the three tiny Farallon Islands outside San Francisco Bay and then the Channel Islands off southern California, and Drake would not have regarded any of these as being capable of sustaining a colony.

John Drake was never heard from again, however, and so it is interesting to compare this information with the earliest known account of Drake's Pacific voyage written in England. An unsigned manuscript known as the "Anonymous Narrative", it is titled *A discourse of Sir Francis Drakes jorney and exploytes ... into Mare de Sur.*[32] Attached to it are some notes written in the same hand and ink, and mention in one of these that Drake's released pilot Nuño da Silva was taken to Spain in 1582 establishes that the narrative could not have been written earlier than 1583. Crossing out of some passages and other evidence in the narrative suggests that it is the first draft of a carefully abridged story, adapted from a journal or deposition taken from a member of Drake's company after their return.[33] Wagner has established that from the Strait of Magellan onward, Richard Hakluyt's eventual published account, "The Famous Voyage", is in turn adapted from this manuscript narrative, except that is, for the voyage north from Guatulco and then on to the Moluccas, where a different story is substituted.[34] Indeed, this *Anonymous Narrative* appears to be written in Hakluyt's own hand, and may in fact be a rare example of his work in manuscript. A detailed palaeographic investigation of this possibility would therefore be of interest, although the result would not alter the conclusions from this study.

Notably, the narrative devotes over 2,000 words to a colourful description of the time Drake spent travelling from the island of Mocha in Chile to Guatulco, but less than 200 words to his journey from Guatulco northward and then across the Pacific to the Moluccas. And especially interesting, where the later, published accounts state that Drake departed from his careenage on 23 July and then made his first landfall in the western Pacific on 30 September, this narrative states that he did not leave the careenage until the end of August, and did not reach the Moluccas until the end of November. The relevant portions of the narrative for this segment of the voyage are:

> here [Guatulco] drake watred his ship & departed sayling northwardes till he came to .48. gr. of the septentrionall Latitud still finding a very lardge sea trending toward the north *but being afraid to spend long time in seeking for the straite hee turned back againe* still keping along the cost as nere land as hee might, vntil hee came to .44. g. and then hee found a harborrow for his ship where he grounded his ship to trim her ... and when they had graved and watred theire ship in the latter ende of August they set sayle and bent their course S.S.W. and had not the sight of land againe till ye latter end of november.[35] (my italics)

Thus, like Madox and John Drake, this narrative places the limit of Drake's northern reach at latitude 48°. And further, it confirms that he was looking for the Strait of Anian. Unlike the later published accounts, however, it states that the harbour where Drake careened his ship was in latitude 44°. And very significantly, it makes no mention of John Drake's islands, or of him naming any place Nova Albion. It appears then that Nova Albion and the harbour where Drake stopped for repairs must have been separate places. And what is most interesting is that the numerals '4' and '8' comprising the latitude of '48' given for Drake's northern reach, are written quite differently from elsewhere in the manuscript.[36]

In 1997 the manuscript was examined utilizing the British Library's *Video Spectral Comparator*, technology which has proven effective in identifying alterations and forgeries of documents. Photographs of the numerals under various light conditions created by this device confirmed that the latitude of Drake's northern reach had been altered by the writer. In a photo labelled 'transmitted light', a triangle of light emitted by the parchment is clearly visible between the curved bowl of a '5' and the vertical and horizontal strokes of the '4' crossing over top of it. Then in another photo a '3' is visible beneath the '8', its bottom stroke truncated so as to be distinguished from an underlying '0' originally written opposite the '5'. Evidently after the '0' was overwritten with the '3', the numeral was transformed again by adding the top loop of the '8'. Originally the writer had noted 50°, and then he had changed this to 53°, and then finally to 48°. Thus, it appears that while reading the journal from which he was adapting his narrative, the writer had been noting Drake's progress northward when he remembered that 48° was as far

Numerals written in the *Anonymous Narrative*

Date of return to England

Latitude given for Drake's northern reach.
Compare the '8' here with that in the date '1580'

Latitude of Drake's careenage.
Note the crisp strokes in the '4's here
in comparison to the '4' in '48'.

The altered numerals viewed in relief
utilizing the 'Video Spectral Comparator'

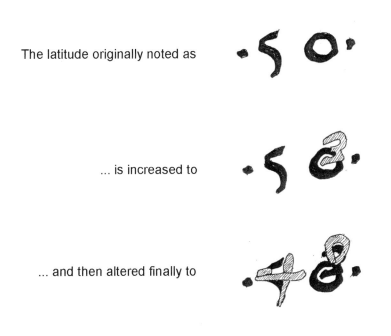

The latitude originally noted as

... is increased to

... and then altered finally to

The sequence of alterations

as he was allowed to say Drake had gone. Here then was an official cutoff point for information about Drake's northern explorations, which must have been established sometime before Madox and the younger Drake left England with Fenton in May 1582, never to return.

But why was the cutoff established at 48°? A glance at a modern map of the coast is all that is required in order to suggest the reason. The 48th parallel crosses the northwest coast of America just 23 miles south of Cape Flattery, which marks a fundamental and dramatic change in the character of the coastline. From Cape Flattery southward the coastline runs virtually unbroken and is devoid of islands or straits. But then at Cape Flattery this unremitting coastline suddenly gives way to the Strait of Juan de Fuca and a great coastal archipelago stretching northwest some 750 miles into southern Alaska—one of the most labyrinthine coastlines in the world. It is easy to see that 48° would have been the logical point to establish a cutoff for information about Drake's explorations, to conceal the existence of islands and straits north of Cape Flattery. And significantly, 50° and 53° which were initially written as his northern reach and then covered over are the latitudes of Vancouver Island and the Queen Charlotte Islands respectively.

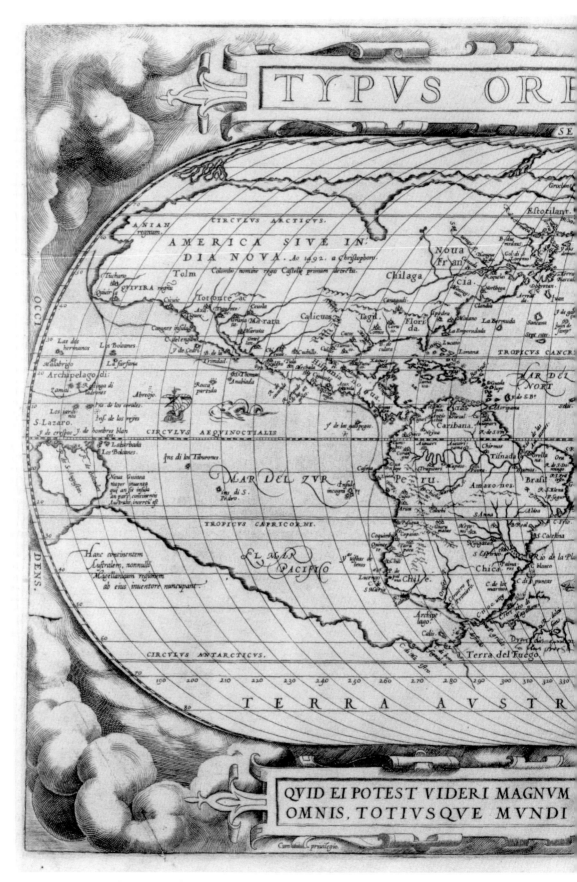

The track of Drake's voyage added in manuscript to a print of Abraham Ortelius' world map, 1579 edition.

By Permission of The British Library

TERRARVM.

EVROPA

Nova Zembla

Noruegia
Suedia
Bergen

Tartaria

Tataia

Tangut · Mongol.

Naiman · Ongul

Cattipara

Cathaio

Russia

ASIA

China.

Turcheltan

Samarhand

Corafan

Persia

Guzarate · India orientalis

AFRICA.
Agi
Tymba

Nubia

Arabia.

Aden

Abissini

Manicon
go.

Melinde

Vasco de Acuña

Due Compagne

Don Garzia

Poueada

ANVS AE
PICVS.

Lantchidol
mare.

Pecan

Iaua minor.

LYCACH

MALETVR

Vaſtiſsimas hic eſse
regiones ex M. Pauli Ven: et
Lud. Varronanni ſcriptis pe
regrinationibus conſtat.

MAR DI INDI

Los Romeros

Iuan de Lisboa.

Pſitacorum regio.
ſic á Luſitanis appellata ob in
credibilē earum auium ſondem
magnitudinem.

Tristan de
Acuña

C. Forno

40 50 60 70 80 90 100 110 120 130 140 150 160 170 180

S NONDVM COGNITA.

ORIENS.

S HVMANIS, CVI AETERNITAS
SIT MAGNITVDO. CICERO:

Hogenbergus ſculpsit

There is no doubt that Drake recorded his navigation and the coasts which he saw in considerable detail and returned to England with many charts, sketches and pictures depicting where he had been.[37] Nuño da Silva said that Drake and his young cousin John, "a great painter", worked late into the nights filling a book with drawings and paintings of everything they saw. And the Spanish nobleman Francisco de Zarate whom Drake briefly detained in Central America was alarmed to find that he was accumulating such accurate details of the coast that no one who used them could possibly go astray.[38] Historian Helen Wallis argues convincingly that the "diary" which Mendoza reported Drake had given to Elizabeth in their first meeting was this illustrated journal, or 'rutter' (from the French term *routier* for route book).[39] Sadly, this precious record of Drake's explorations appears to be lost forever. However, as will be seen there are indications that Drake kept copies of some of the drawings. Mendoza also reported that Drake had presented the Queen with a very large map in that meeting, and Wallis suggests that it was this item which Samuel Purchas described in 1625 as "the Map of Sir Francis Drakes Voyage presented to Queen Elizabeth, still hanging in His Majesties Gallerie at White Hall neere the Privie Chamber". This item is thought to have been lost in the fire that destroyed the Palace of Whitehall in 1698.[40] But Purchas also described this map as containing a portrait of Elizabeth and Latin inscriptions, and said that "the name Elizabeth is expressed in golden letters, with a gold Crowne, Garter and Armes affixed", and it is difficult to believe that Drake would have returned with a map containing such decorative refinements.

However, there is in the British Library what appears to be the earliest surviving map depicting Drake's route around the world. This is a print of the 1579 edition of Ortelius' *Typus Orbis Terrarum,* on which Drake's route has been drawn in manuscript.[41] Following his route southward toward Magellan's Strait, two little ships are drawn opposite the Argentine coast. These represent vessels which Drake abandoned en route. In subsequent maps the concept is enhanced by also depicting the number of vessels that remained, which diminishes eventually to one ship as Drake's track continues into the Pacific. Below the extremity of South America there is a manuscript note concerning his naming of the islands south of Magellan's Strait after Elizabeth, and this too is refined in the later maps. It therefore appears that someone who was privy to the details of the voyage was considering here, probably for the first time, the design of a map to commemorate Drake's voyage, and the possibility of adapting Ortelius' map for the purpose. Then, Drake's track continues steadily northward in the Pacific, reaching past Ortelius' great westward bulge in North America … to latitude 57°.

CHAPTER THREE

Islands of Good Land

When Edward Fenton reached England in May 1583 Elizabeth had him arrested for not continuing the voyage. It likely was not long afterward that Drake began manoeuvring again for permission to lead a new expedition out to the Pacific himself. In November, Walsingham uncovered Spanish plans to invade England, and if Drake had not already begun lobbying the Queen he would have seen the opportunity to do so at that point. Then in June 1584 Elizabeth's hopes for a new alliance with France were dashed when her suitor, the Duke of Anjou, died suddenly; and the following month the leader of the Dutch liberation forces, William of Orange, was assassinated by a Spanish agent. Resistance to the Spanish occupation of the Netherlands was wavering, and it was feared that it might collapse altogether. Leicester and Walsingham persuaded Elizabeth that she had to put on a show of force, and Drake's project, which doubtless had been under discussion for some time, finally surfaced. On 29 July 1584 she agreed to invest £17,000 toward equipping Drake's proposed expedition for 'the Moluccas'.[1]

The plan of the voyage called for eleven ships, four barks, twenty pinnaces and 1600 men.[2] If anything, Drake certainly was persistent. Undoubtedly this was the same project he had proposed in 1580. Nor can there be any doubt that then and now his real aim was to disrupt the flow of South American treasure from which Philip was financing his growing aggression. Very probably Drake was intent on sacking Panama. But what about completing the discovery of the northwest passage, did this still figure in his plan? It surely must have in preference to returning via Magellan's Strait or sailing all the way around the world again. And with a fleet then reinforced via the passage and operating from Nova Albion, Englishmen could continue to plunder Spain's Pacific commerce with comparative ease. Here then was Drake's grand vision for the South Sea enterprise: a secret naval base from which they would intercept Philip's treasure shipments from Peru, Chile and the Philippines and send them home via the northwest passage. Especially vulnerable would be the Manila Galleons returning across the North Pacific to the Californias with rich cargoes of gold, silks and gems from the Orient.

Elizabeth signed Drake's commission on Christmas eve 1584, but soon afterward she began to reconsider.[3] Most probably she began to feel uneasy about Drake taking so many ships and experienced men away on such a long voyage when the Spanish invasion fleet might soon appear off England's shores. And so, in the spring Drake's objective was changed to the Caribbean. No doubt the reasoning was that he could sail at the end of the summer, which was the projected season for the invasion, sack Philip's Caribbean possessions and possibly even intercept his gold fleet, and yet still be home in time to help combat any invasion attempt the following summer. Drake, who was now eager for action, embraced the plan although no doubt he was disappointed that he was unable to prosecute his grand scheme for the Pacific.

In the meanwhile Walsingham was scrambling to develop a new alliance against Spain. Especially important was the position France would take in the growing confrontation. Richard Hakluyt was now working in Paris, ostensibly as secretary to English ambassador Sir Edward Stafford, but also gathering intelligence about French activities in the New World for Walsingham.[4] In Paris Hakluyt found there was much curiosity and speculation about Drake's great voyage. On 16 October 1584, ambassador Stafford wrote to Walsingham

> I find from Mr. Haklitt that Drakes journey is kept very secret in England, but here is in everyones mouth. When questioned about it, I have answered as an ignorant body, as indeed I am, except for what I find by their speeches here. It may [be] they hit not all right, but they guess in great part.[5]

Then in March 1585, perhaps coincidentally but rather suspiciously so, Walsingham received a letter from Henry of Navarre, Protestant heir to the throne of France, requesting the "collection", meaning presumably the charts, and the "discourse" of Drake's voyage.[6] What was fortuitous about Henry's request was that it created for Walsingham the opportunity for a dialogue around the possibility of a new alliance, beginning with their mutual interest in rejecting Spain's avowed monopoly over the New World. The suggestion then is that he may have had someone, possibly even Hakluyt, plant the idea of Henry making his request in order to open up this avenue of discussion.

In all events, receipt of a map "many coloured and gilded" was soon acknowledged by Henry,[7] and with it presumably he received a 'discourse' of the voyage. Indeed the *Anonymous Narrative*, being titled *A discourse of Drake's journey and exploytes ... into Mare de Sur*, may well have been the first draft of the requested account. And notably, Hakluyt returned, or was recalled to London for a month shortly after Walsingham received Henry's request, so he could well have been the author.[8] That the government was now willing to provide an account of Drake's voyage to certain persons for propaganda purposes was then confirmed by a note added to a Privy Council memorandum on negotiations with Germany and Denmark later that year: "And the Landgrave of Hesse having asked for a discourse touching Sir Francis Drake's first voyage, his request should be satisfied."[9] Thus, it was no longer a matter of no information being given out, but rather what was to be provided and to whom. In March 1585, however, Walsingham would have had little

Sir Francis Walsingham, by John de Critz

By Permission of the National Portrait Gallery

time to spare for overseeing the design of a map which depicted Drake's voyage, and indeed it may have been unnecessary for him to do so. It appears that Drake had already begun having a few maps drawn for presentation privately to important people, as it is recorded that he had presented one similarly described as "richly decorated with coloured and gilded designs" to the Archbishop of Canterbury.[10]

Unfortunately both Henry's and the Archbishop's maps are now lost. However, the manuscript known as the Drake Mellon map, although not decorated with gold leaf, almost certainly is another in this series. Its title, in Latin, translates:

A true description of the naval expedition of Francis Drake, Englishman and Knight, who with five ships departed from the western part of England on 13 December 1577, circumnavigated the globe and returned on 26 September 1580 with one ship remaining, the others having been destroyed by waves or fire.

This and the scenes in the corners, which depict events that occurred on the voyage, establish that the map's original purpose was solely to commemorate Drake's voyage around the world. In the lower left corner, Drake's arrival at the island of Ternate in the Moluccas is depicted, and in the lower right corner, the *Golden Hinde* is shown stuck on a reef near Celebes. Then some time later the route of his 1585-86 Caribbean expedition has been added. As this was likely done soon after Drake's return from that voyage, it is a reasonable supposition that the map was drawn in its original state sometime before he sailed for the Caribbean in September 1585. On the voyage Drake sacked Santo Domingo, Cartagena and St. Augustine and then stopped to rescue the bedraggled survivors of the first attempt to found the colony of Virginia. Thus the flag and inscription about Virginia has been added, and possibly also the boundary separating North America from New Spain, after his return. Quite obviously the map is an unabashed exercise in self-promotion by Drake, illustrating the development of England's overseas interests as being synonymous with his expeditions.

Let us therefore imagine the removal of Drake's 1585-86 exploit and focus on the original scheme of the map. Overall, the configuration of the continents and the major rivers bears a resemblance to Ortelius' world map except for the Pacific coast of North America, where his prominent continental bulge has been removed. In northeast America a flag and a small opening in the coast indicate the location of *Meta Incognita*, although this is placed in longitude 15 degrees east of its true location. Then, marking Drake's track southward to the Strait of Magellan there is the scheme of little ships first contemplated in the map previously examined, and in the legend below is the inscription concerning the *Elizabetha Islands*. Drake's track then runs northward in the Pacific until it reaches a landfall, at precisely latitude 40°, on the outside of a southward-pointing peninsula before heading southwest across the Pacific. Nearby, an English flag is planted, again at 40°, at the head of the inlet behind the peninsula, and an inscription explains that Drake discovered this place and named it Nova Albion in 1579.

Nova Albion on the Drake Mellon Map

Courtesy of the Yale Center for British Art, Paul Mellon Collection

Of particular interest, the Drake Mellon map is one of the earliest to depict a boundary separating North America from New Spain. The other map which shares this distinction is the French Drake map, so named because the inscriptions are in that language. The dimensions and basic scheme of the map are identical, and so it appears to be another of Drake's private maps. Curiously however, it appears to have been drawn by a different artist and it has a rather unfinished look. Several of the placenames are incomplete or misspelled, and strangely, the inscription noting Drake's discovery of Nova Albion is placed adjacent to Greenland. These aspects together with cruder rendering of the corner scenes suggest that it is a rough copy of one of Drake's maps. Nevertheless it was engraved in this state by a Nicola van Sype, whose name appears in the lower right corner. The reason, it appears, is the legend along the bottom margin, "Carte veuee et corige par le dict Siegneur drack" ('map seen and corrected by Sir Drake'). A family of engravers by the name of van Sype is known to have been active in Germany in the first decades of the seventeenth century[11], and the surviving copies of the map were all found in either the 1627 or 1641 edition of the French translation of Hakluyt's account of Drake's voyage.[12] Thus, it appears that the person who obtained this copy of one of Drake's maps subsequently showed it to him and then added this note. Then sometime later, probably after this person's death, someone decided because of the note concerning Drake to have it faithfully copied, and asked van Sype to do so.[13]

The addition of a portrait of Drake with an inscription stating that he is 42 years of age suggests that the original map from which it was copied was presented to someone who had never met him. Then there are the boundaries in North America. First there is a line across the continent, expressing the desire to contain the Spanish to the south. Then there is a boundary around New France indicating a wish to acknowledge, but also to contain France's claim to part of North America. This fits the picture we have of Walsingham inviting a dialogue with Henry of Navarre about the future of North America. Also, the boundaries leave a space on the Atlantic coast which evidently is reserved for England, but which is not yet named Virginia. And notably, the reconnaissance of that coast to select a site for the colony occurred in the summer of 1584, and then the colony was established in the summer of 1585. It therefore appears that the original from which this map was copied was drawn sometime between those dates. This coupled with the portrait and the inscriptions in French leaves little room for doubt that the map is a copy of the one which was sent to Henry of Navarre in the spring of 1585.

Most interesting of all, however, are the changes to the scheme of Drake's voyage to northwest America. In this map his track continues northward past a series of islands to latitude 48°, where an inscription states "Tournede la acanst de la glasse" ('turned back because of the ice'), and then it returns southward and stops, again precisely at 40°, at one of the islands before heading across the Pacific. Thus,

The Drake Mellon map, 1585 – 1586
Manuscript in pen, ink and wash on vellum (44 x 24 cm.)

what was represented as a peninsula in the Drake Mellon map has now become an island, one of a chain of four islands stretching northwest along the coast some 500 miles in the scale of the map. Here then is corroboration of John Drake's testimony about the discovery of several 'islands of good land', except however that Herrera's version of his testimony was that Drake named the largest of the islands Nova Albion, whereas the map shows him stopping at the smallest of the islands. And the chain of islands runs from 38° to 45°, where in reality there are no such islands. However, it does appear that Drake seized the opportunity presented by Henry of Navarre's request to reveal considerably more about his explorations than he had in his previous maps.

Then there is a third map of this genre, known as the Dutch Drake map because most of the inscriptions are in that language. The sole surviving specimen was bound with a copy of the Latin account of Drake's 1585 Caribbean voyage, published at Leyden in 1588. Clearly this is the finished item intended by the person, evidently a Dutch mapmaker, who obtained the copy of Henry of Navarre's map and showed it to Drake. It follows then that Drake's suggested corrections should be incorporated in this map, and indeed there are two significant changes. The one which is immediately apparent is the introduction of a northwest passage reaching across the top of America, implying a potential junction with the Strait of Anian somewhere beneath the scrollwork in the corner of the map. At the Atlantic entrance to the passage are the six islands labelled Meta Incognita in George Best's 1578 world map. The second change can be seen only on closer examination. In northwest America the scheme of Drake's explorations is unchanged from the French Drake map except for one detail: the island where his track stops has now been redrawn to become the largest in the chain. Here then is corroboration of John Drake's testimony that Drake named the largest island Nova Albion. It very much appears that Drake did in fact see and correct the French Drake map sometime before 1588.

There is also a solitary example of the Dutch Drake map in a second state (not shown), which was bound in a copy of the German account of Drake's Caribbean voyage, published in 1589.[14] In this, Drake's track in the North Pacific has been extended further, although rather strangely in that it veers westward toward Japan. It appears that the engraver wished to indicate that Drake had gone further north, but was unable to do so because the space in the map is occupied by the vignette of the *Golden Hinde* and the scrollwork beneath the main legend.

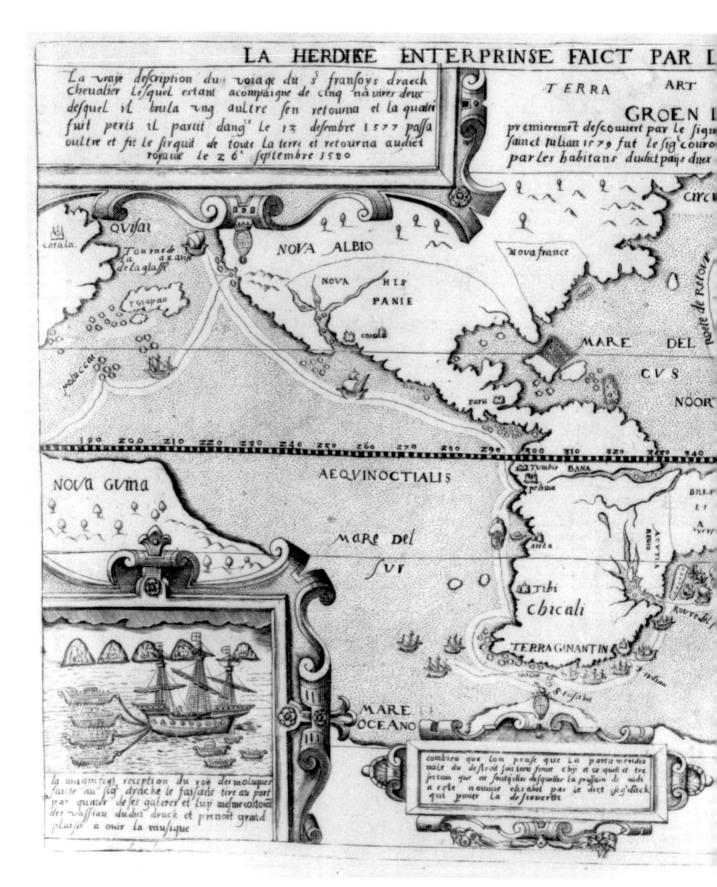

The French Drake map, circa 1585
Printed (44 x 24 cm.)

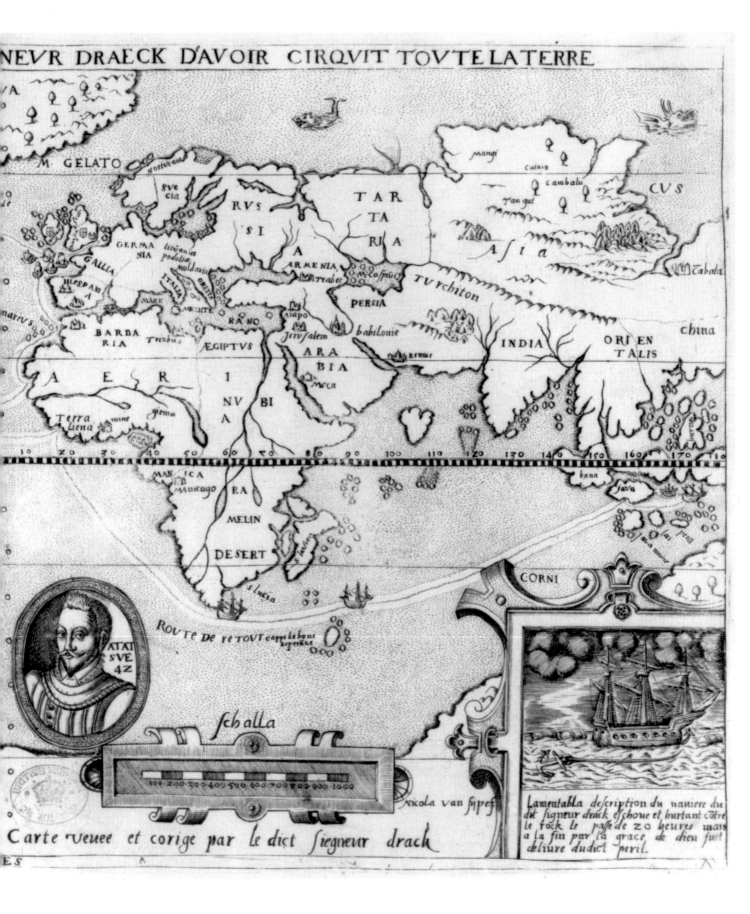

NEVR DRAECK D'AVOIR CIRQVIT TOVTE LA TERRE

M. GELATO

SVECIA

RVSSIA

TARTARIA

mangi
Cataio
Cambalu
Tangut
CVS

GERMANIA
Lituania podolia
moldavia

ASIA

Tabata

GALLIA
ITALIA

ARMENIA
Trabes
M. Cospiu

TVrchiton

HISPANIA
MARE

RANO

Alapo

PERSIA

china

MELITE

Jerusalem

babilonie

canarius

BARBARIA
Trobus

EGIPTVS
Remus
INDIA
ORIENTALIS

AERI
N
V
 ARABIA
Meca

Terra dena
mine
genua

NUBIA

MANICA
Mancago
RA
MELIN
bana
java

DESERT

s. lucia

CORNI

ROVTE DE RETOVT cappe le bont esperence

ÆTATIS SVE 42

schalla

100 200 300 400 500 600 700 800 900 1000

Carte veuee et corige par le dict sieigneur drach

Lamentabla description du naviere du dit signeur drack eschoue et hurtant contre le rock le passe de 20 heures mais a la fin par la grace de dieu fut delivre dudict peril.

LA HERDIKE INTERPRINSE FAICT PAR LE SIGNE

TERA FORM

ASTOTELAN

TERA NOVA

NOVA ALBIA

NOVA FRANCIA

Catala
Quinsai
Tournel
La Mente
D. La palse
Tgiapan

NOV A HISPA NIA
Canola

FLORIDA

INDIA

OCCI
Zaru

DEN TALIS

NOVA GUINA

CIRC. ÆQVINOCTIALIS

MARE DEL

SVR

Primero

PERV

Arica

B ACVI STIA REG IO

Molucke

Chile

CHICA REGIO GIGANTIV M

R. del

S. Elisabel
TE RADELF

EST R HO DE M GALLA

The Dutch Drake map, 1588
Printed (45 x 24 cm)

TERA FVRMA

PICMEOS

NOVA ZEMBLA

Groen

Mangi

Cataio

Fergat

CA Cabal

Colgoio

NORWEGIA

Cana Picora

TARTARIA

Tanguc

Colmogra

VE SVEG IA

RVS SIA

OR P

JAIO

ARMENIA

ASIA

Cambalum

GERMA NIA

FRANCIA

ASIA MINOR

Trabet

MAR CASPO

TVRC

Cambalum

HISP

ITA

Ioppe

PERSIA

HITON

CHINA

ANIA

BARBA

Ierusalane

Babilo nien

INDIA

OR IENT

RIA Tripeli

EGIPTA

Ormus

ALIS

AFRICA

ARABIA Mecha

Goa

C. de Verd

NVBIA

Calacuc

Mijnne

Genee

Salen

CE

35° 34° 33° 32° 3 30° 21 29 20 26 19 24 23 22 21 20 1

S mari

Bann

Java

Manicon gue

MELINDE

Sint

V S

Java minor

Pera

Lowren

S. helena

G. de bon S. luci
Spe ri

Route de retoue

A N

SCALA MILIAR
100 200 300 400 500 600 700 800 900 1000

Beschrininge vant tschip van Draeck
Stootende 20 uren Lanck tegens een
Clip die de heere daer na weer verlost heft
Comme le Vaisseau du Cap.ne Draeck a
Couru grand peril 20 heures de long

What is striking about the long chain of islands on these maps is that although the latitudes are wrong, there is the unmistakable impression that Drake has formed a comprehension of the great coastal archipelago extending northward from Cape Flattery that the explorers who reached the region two centuries later acquired only after numerous expeditions. The first explorers of record were the Spaniards Juan Perez in 1774 and Bodega y Quadra in 1775, but they saw only the outer coast and did not realize that it was comprised of large islands screening a complex inner coast. Then Captain James Cook spent a month at Nootka Sound in 1778 without realizing that it was part of a large island. As the maritime fur trade developed, Captain George Dixon circumnavigated the Queen Charlotte Islands and others found the openings at the north and south ends of Vancouver Island. But it was not until 1792, when Dionisio Galiano and George Vancouver jointly charted narrow Johnstone Strait leading westward from the 'Gulf' (Strait) of Georgia back into the Pacific that Vancouver Island was finally delineated, and then it took two more years before the principal islands at the northern end of the archipelago were charted. Granted Vancouver and the Spanish worked their way methodically up the coast, surveying and charting every inlet to its end, whereas Drake could have conducted a fast-paced reconnaissance, following the general trend of the coast rather than investigating every inlet. However, it is clear from the later explorations that in order to have identified these islands as such, Drake had to have sailed the length of the straits separating them from the mainland. Therefore, it should be possible to match some aspect of the inner coast as depicted in Drake's maps with the actual coastline.

It is important to appreciate that the islands are drawn at a very small scale, and in order for them to be distinguished at this scale the spaces between them and the continental mainland are bound to have been exaggerated, and therefore to appear distorted when magnified. Nevertheless, the islands are fitted into the coast in a particular way which suggests that Drake had first-hand knowledge of its complexity. The key is the island where Drake's track stops on the Dutch Drake map, which has been redrawn so that it becomes the largest in the chain. Vancouver Island is in fact the largest in the archipelago, and so it is reasonable to begin by placing the two side by side. Johnstone Strait, which separates northern Vancouver Island from the mainland runs nearly east-west, and looking at Drake's corrected map it is clear that care has been taken to define this feature. Moreover, the island has a concave east coast and a distinctive southern tip resembling Vancouver Island. The way the island and the strait are redrawn, it appears that the detail has been transposed from a larger sketch by Drake. Now the identity of the two large embayments in the mainland coast opposite becomes clear. The one at the eastern end of what would be Johnstone Strait, although somewhat exaggerated, could only be Desolation Sound. And the one opposite the southern tip of the island would be the line of mountains behind the Fraser River estuary. Notably, the later Spanish

Identification of Drake's Islands

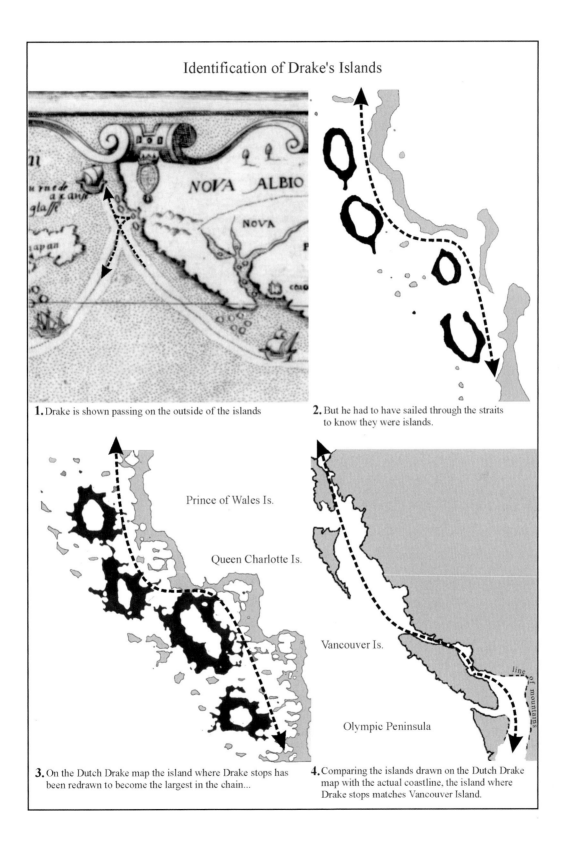

1. Drake is shown passing on the outside of the islands

2. But he had to have sailed through the straits to know they were islands.

Prince of Wales Is.

Queen Charlotte Is.

Vancouver Is.

Olympic Peninsula

line of mountains

3. On the Dutch Drake map the island where Drake stops has been redrawn to become the largest in the chain...

4. Comparing the islands drawn on the Dutch Drake map with the actual coastline, the island where Drake stops matches Vancouver Island.

explorers also thought that this was a large bay marked by the mountains to the north and east. Thus, it appears that Drake must have sailed the length of the straits separating Vancouver Island from the mainland.

Then, the two islands to the north are offset to the west and aligned as they should be to represent the Queen Charlottes, undoubtedly seen as a single island, and further north, Prince of Wales Island. Therefore, Drake must have sailed the length of the straits, now known as the Inside Passage, at least as far as the northern extremity of Prince of Wales Island, at latitude 56° 20' in southern Alaska. But what would explain the configuration of the coast to the south of Vancouver Island, including another large island where there is none? Using the coast mountain ranges to mark the mainland coast, as it appears he did at the mouth of the Fraser River, Drake would have found that from there southward the mountains step to the east, and seeing the widely separated mountains of the Olympic Peninsula he must have speculated that it too might be an island.

Now it becomes clear that there was another coverup rule besides the 48° cutoff for information about Drake's explorations. The additional rule was designed to conceal the location of the secret colony site. Let us review. First, the Drake Mellon map shows Drake making his landfall at precisely latitude 40° on the outside of a peninsula. However, in the French Drake map this peninsula becomes an island, again at 40°, and then in the Dutch Drake map the island is redrawn so that it becomes recognizable as Vancouver Island, which is actually centred at latitude 50°. Notably also, this is the first latitude written and then covered over in the *Anonymous Narrative*. It appears then that Drake made his initial landfall on the outer coast of Vancouver Island. Returning to the Drake Mellon map however, this shows the flag planted not on the outer coast of the peninsula but rather at the head of the inlet behind it, and again at 40°. And since it is now revealed that this peninsula is actually Vancouver Island and we are told that Drake gave the name Nova Albion to the largest of the islands he discovered, it appears that he must have selected a site for the future colony on the shores of the Strait of Georgia, on the east coast of Vancouver Island, near latitude 50°.

Clearly then, these schemes in Drake's maps depicting his northern explorations are cryptograms which have been carefully contrived to place his secret colony site 10 degrees south of its true location. Thus England could claim possession of the territory without exposing the future colony to attack by the Spanish. But what is most interesting is that Drake took the liberty of enhancing the cryptogram in the map which was sent to Henry of Navarre, and then sometime prior to 1588, when nothing of the sort was yet allowed to be published in England, he provided a further significant enhancement of the information to a Dutch cartographer.

CHAPTER FOUR

Leaked Information

Drake's 1585 Caribbean expedition seems to mark a significant political change around his scheme for a grand Pacific project. Up to this point he clearly had taken a proprietary interest in the various plans and proposals to follow up on his vital discovery. But allowing that he had been absent from England for ten months, he must have been surprised to learn when he reached Plymouth in July 1586 that a new expedition had departed for the Pacific under the command of young Thomas Cavendish just a few days previous. When Drake sailed for the Caribbean in September 1585 Cavendish was at sea with Richard Grenville's expedition to set up the colony of Virginia. No doubt because of the continuing secrecy around the project, little has been found concerning the organization of Cavendish's Pacific voyage. Just 26 years of age, he had been educated at Cambridge and the Inns of Court and was related to many of the prominent men surrounding Elizabeth. Leicester had been in the Netherlands since the previous December and the Queen's cousin Lord Hunsdon appears to have had a hand in the project. And, of course, Elizabeth undoubtedly had a financial stake in the expedition.

If he had not already been told prior to his departure in 1585, certainly Drake must now have realized that Elizabeth had no intention of allowing him to embark on another voyage to the Pacific while there was any threat of a Spanish attempt to invade England. She could spare a young adventurer like Cavendish for the purpose, but not her most able naval commander. Drake's focus must now be on strategies and actions to address the growing menace to England herself, and this was a challenge which he took up energetically. At the same time however, it is clear that he was eager to return to the Pacific, and it could not have been easy for him to accept that the opportunity had been handed to someone else. It is a reasonable supposition then that he now sought permission to publish a map and an account like those which had been sent to the Protestant princes, in order that he might at least receive credit for the extraordinary reconnaissance which he had performed to lay the foundation for the enterprise. And as will be seen, there are indications that he was given to understand he would be allowed to do so. But since Cavendish was now headed for the Pacific and might be endangered by publication of any details of his voyage, it is also reasonable to suppose that he was told that he would have to wait until Cavendish returned.

In mid October 1586 Drake sailed for the Netherlands seeking to enlist Dutch support for a joint naval operation against Spain. He spent several weeks there, and this may be when he met the Dutch cartographer who had obtained a copy of Henry

of Navarre's map. It is unclear whether he was this person, but within a few months
thereafter Abraham Ortelius began revising his atlas maps to incorporate new
information in northwest America, and while the toponyms are in Spanish, there can
be no question of their relationship to Drake's voyage. Ortelius had begun writing to
his contacts in England for information about the voyage soon after Drake's return.
On 12 December 1580 Ortelius' colleague Gerard Mercator had written, thanking
him for

> the dispatch about the new English voyage on which you have previously
> sent me a report through Rumold [Mercator's son] ... I am persuaded that
> there can be no reason for so carefully concealing the course followed during
> this voyage, or for putting out differing accounts of the route taken and the
> areas visited, other than that they may have found very wealthy regions never
> yet discovered by Europeans.[1]

Ortelius had a large network of information gatherers, and whether it was he or
one of his associates who copied Henry of Navarre's map and eventually made
contact with Drake, either through Leicester in the Netherlands or through an
intermediary in London, is still open to conjecture, but clearly he was eager to
incorporate some of Drake's information in his maps. In all probability, discussion
of Henry of Navarre's map with Drake led to a promise by him to supply more
information in the form of revisions to Ortelius' maps. In any case, to his map of the
world Ortelius now added Drake's chain of islands, placing them much further
north, and between latitudes 57° and 58° he added a *R. de los estrechos* or 'river of
the straits'[2], and then at 54° a cape *Mendocino*. Then, far to the south at 40°—
precisely the latitude where Drake's maps show him stopping pursuant to the ten
degree coverup rule—Ortelius added a *Baya de Pinaz* or 'bay of small ships'. And
on his map of the Americas (not shown), he added *Grandes Corrientes* or 'strong
currents' at latitude 54°; another *R. de los estrechos* at 49°; *C. de Trabaios* or 'cape
of worries' at 48°; and then further south, on the underside of his westward-bulging
coastline, a *Rio Grande*. Curiously however, although Ortelius' revised maps were
engraved in 1587, very few prints from the new plates were incorporated in the
many atlases which he sold between then and 1589, and the new world map did not
become a regular inclusion in his atlas until 1592.[3] The suggestion then, is that he
had undertaken not to release the revised maps until he received further word in that
connection.

There is a world map which was included in some copies of Richard Hakluyt's
Principall Navigations in 1589 which suggests something more about the sequence
of events. The map is a rather poor copy of Ortelius' now familiar *Typus Orbis
Terrarum* and contains exactly the same details in northwest America as Ortelius
added by way of revisions to his map in 1587. It has generally been regarded as an

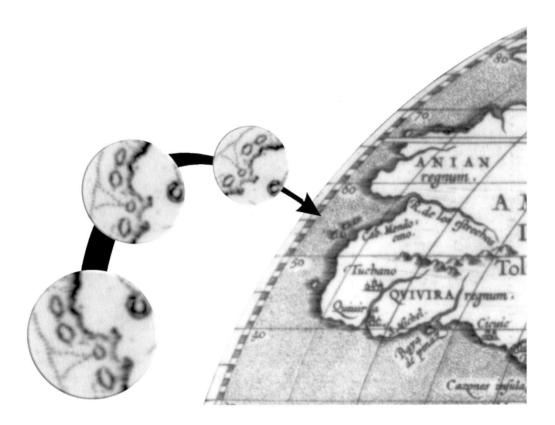

Drake's islands appear on Abraham Ortelius' 1587 world map

English copy of Ortelius' 1587 map, and Wagner asserts that it was engraved by Flemish engraver Jodocus Hondius, who was then residing in London.[4]   Notably however, its corners are decorated with clouds as in the earlier editions of Ortelius' map, the title and main legend are the same as in that edition, and in the southwest Pacific the newly introduced Solomon Islands are placed among the old inscriptions adjacent to New Guinea.[5]   Also faintly visible in the map are boundaries in North America like those in the Drake Mellon map and the French Drake map.   Then in Ortelius' 1587 map decorative medallions are substituted for the clouds in the corners, the word *AETERNITAS* is split in the main legend at the bottom, and the old inscriptions adjacent to New Guinea are removed to clear the space for the Solomons.   It therefore appears that Ortelius' revisions may actually have been taken from this modified version of his earlier edition which was produced in England in late 1586 or early 1587 and later inserted in Hakluyt's book.

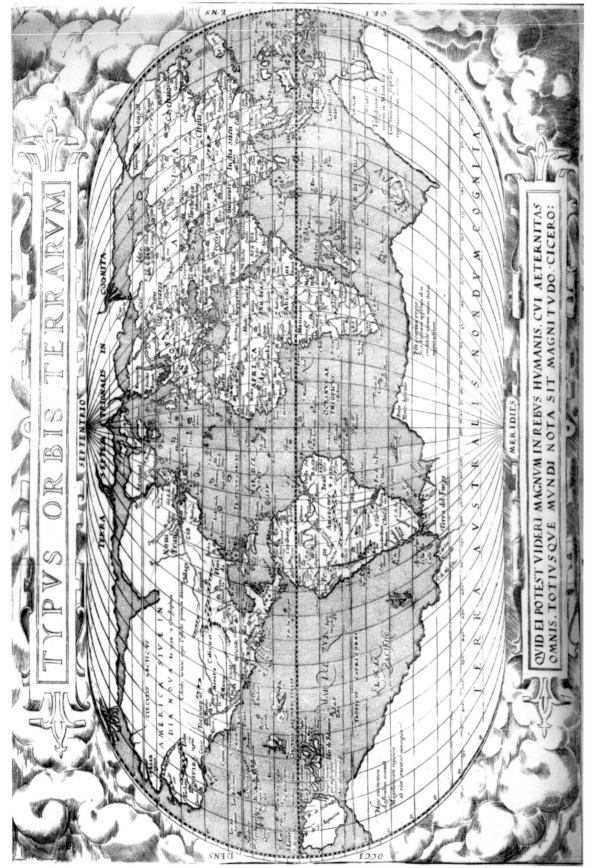

The world map which Richard Hakluyt inserted in *Principall Navigations* is based on Ortelius' 1570 edition with Drake's islands and other information on the Northwest Coast of America as well as the Solomon Islands added.

By Permission of The British Library

Ortelius' revised world map, engraved in 1587, incorporates the same new information found in the map used by Hakluyt, but the clouds in the corners are replaced by medallions, the word AETERNITAS in the main legend is split, and some inscriptions have been removed to clear space around the Solomon Islands.

By Permission of The British Library

Wagner's belief that Jodocus Hondius engraved the English version of Ortelius' map is worthy of further consideration. Hondius emigrated from his native Flanders in 1583 to escape religious persecution by the Spanish, and resided in London for a decade before moving to Amsterdam, where he quickly established himself as one of the Netherlands' most prolific cartographers. Yet, little is known about his work in England prior to 1589. However, a contemporary biography states that while there he "drew many fine draughts and master peeces as Sr Francis Drakes voyage around the world".[6] Also, there is an engraved portrait of Drake (see the frontespiece to this book) which is attributed to Hondius and which contains an inscription stating that it was drawn "from the life" at age 43.[7] Allowing that the map which was sent to Henry of Navarre in the spring of 1585 evidently stated that Drake was 42 at that time, Hondius probably engraved this portrait soon after Drake returned from the Caribbean in 1586. Hondius' most famous work is his splendid Drake Broadside map, to be discussed later. However, comparison of the decorative scrollwork and the scenes in its corners with those in the Drake Mellon map suggests that both maps are by the same artist. It appears then that Hondius' Broadside map is the ultimate rendition of Drake's commemorative map, and that Drake may have employed him in the production of all his maps, including those given to the Archbishop of Canterbury and Henry of Navarre, beginning soon after he arrived in London.

At this juncture Richard Hakluyt was still residing in Paris, where he was printing a new edition of Peter Martyr's celebrated work, *Decades of the New World*. Then in May 1587 he inserted in the book an extraordinary map of the New World. The legend at the bottom of the map states that it was engraved in Paris by "F.G.S.", possibly standing for 'Filips Galle Sculptor'[8], but it is obvious that Hakluyt could not have published it without permission from Walsingham.[9] Notably, the concept of the map is very similar to the Drake Mellon map, except that it omits the track of Drake's voyage. Inscriptions indicate the same four English claims in America, and John Cabot's discovery of Newfoundland in 1496 is noted as well. As this is the earliest known printed map depicting them, it appears that Walsingham had decided to publicize England's territorial claims in the New World. What is interesting is that *Meta Incognita* is placed very near its correct latitude and longitude, and in northwest America *Nova Albion* is inscribed at its true latitude of 50°. Beyond, the coast runs northwest and north, and then at about 56° it begins to curl toward Asia, much as the actual coast of Alaska does.

Equally remarkable is the correction in the longitude of the northwest coast of America. While Ortelius continued to project the coast nearly 195° west of England, Hakluyt's map places Nova Albion just 140° west of England—a correction of more than 2,500 miles—so that the coast bears a closer resemblance to the actual than on any map that would be produced for two centuries thereafter. Wagner suggests that

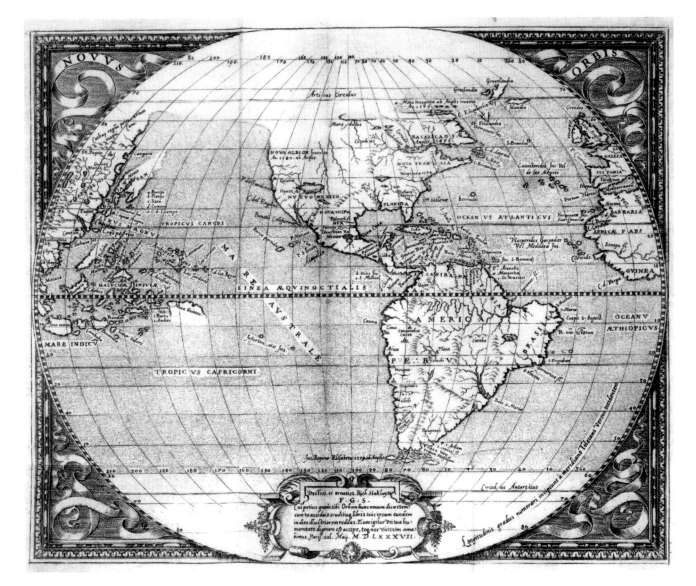

Richard Hakluyt's *Novus Orbis* map, 1587

Courtesy of the Huntington Library

Hakluyt's map was derived from a Spanish map because the prime meridian runs through Toledo.[10] If so, then clearly the archipelago at the extremity of South America and the trend of the northwest coast of America above latitude 43°, which are Drake's discoveries, have been added by Walsingham's cartographer. Still, this does not entirely dispose of the longitude question, because two other English maps which predate this one also place the northwest coast of America 140° west of England: that of Michael Lok previously examined, and a polar projection by John Dee[11], both produced in 1582. It appears then that the question of its longitude may have been resolved by Drake on his voyage.

In 1588 Michael Mercator, grandson of the famous geographer, was given a grant from parliamentary funds[12], most probably by Walsingham, to engrave a silver medallion map commemorating Drake's voyage. The medallion was completed in mid 1589, and it appears that its issue was intended to coincide with the account of Drake's voyage which Hakluyt promised to include in *Principall Navigations,* printed in that same year. As this medallion is the earliest known map of the voyage to be published in England, it is interesting to compare it with Hakluyt's 1587 map. The configuration of South America is identical, as is the east coast of North America. Clearly then, the medallion is derived from Hakluyt's map. On the northwest coast Drake's track runs north to latitude 48°, where *Nova Albion* is inscribed as on his private maps. Thus, the 48 degree cutoff rule is respected. His track then reverses southward to a point opposite the mouth of an inlet, at latitude 38°, before setting off across the Pacific. The inlet runs northward to 40°, implying that Drake reached that point. Obviously this is the same inlet that is depicted in the Drake Mellon map, which we now know is actually the straits beginning at Cape Flattery, latitude 48°, and running north to 50°, where Drake proposed to establish his colony. Thus, the 10 degree rule for concealing its true location is respected. Evidently the inlet cryptogram was preferred to showing the islands because the latter revealed the continuation of the straits northward beyond the colony site. However, it appears that yet another rule has been imposed. Notwithstanding that this map clearly is derived from Hakluyt's, the northwest coast is now moved in longitude from 140° west of England to 170° west (England is located on the reverse side of the medallion). There can be little doubt then that this was a deliberate alteration designed to further obscure Drake's discoveries.

It has been suggested that Hondius may have had a hand in the design of the medallion map, and this is quite plausible as he very likely was by now developing the double-hemisphere design for his Drake Broadside map.[13] However, he was also engaged in the production of another map. There are two engraved versions of the map, one by Hondius and the other by Ortelius, both dated 1589, but again there can be no doubt of the source.[14] As Hondius' map reveals the open sea passage

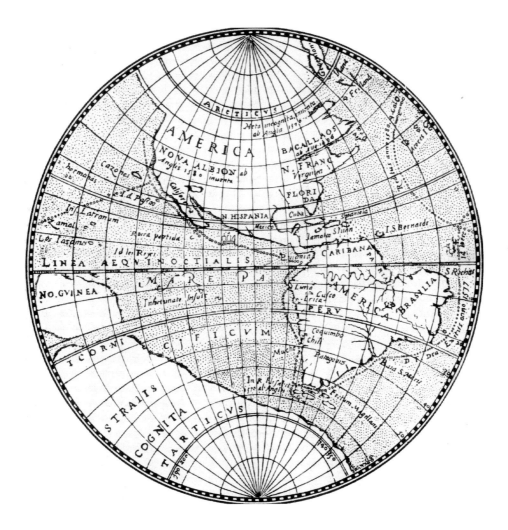

The Silver Medallion map of Drake's voyage, 1589
A paper impression taken from the medal. Actual diameter 6.8 cm.

discovered by Drake south of Tierra del Fuego whereas Ortelius' map does not, it appears that both are derived from a third map which was sent to Ortelius, and which is now lost. In the two printed maps however, the toponyms on the northwest coast are identical, beginning with *Grandes Corrientes* at about latitude 55°, and then followed by a *R. de los estrechos* at 53°, *C. de Trabaios* near 50°, *C. Mendocino* at 48°, *Costa brava* at 46°, and *Baia hermosa* at 44°. Notably, this last toponym, 'beautiful bay', is placed in the same latitude that the *Anonymous Narrative* gives as the location of Drake's careenage. Then, beginning at 40° and continuing down the coast on the underside of Ortelius' great westward bulge, where the latitudes are fictitious, are the following toponyms:

Toponym	Translation
Baia de los pinas	bay of small ships
Mozzo (sic) hermosa	beautiful young women
P. de Sardines	point of small fish
P. St. Michel	point of St. Michael
Baia de los isleos*	bay of islands
B. hermosa	beautiful bay
Plaia	beach
Rio Grande	great river
La tierra brava	rugged land
Punta de pocicion	point of position
Baia de los Pinas	bay of small ships
Baia de fuegos	bay of fires
Rio Bravo	wild river

* placed at the mouth of a large, double-channelled river

After these there is a space and then the placenames are more dispersed. Therefore, these places appear to belong to a distinct group which, for future reference, we shall call Drake's 'southern nomenclature', as distinct from the places previously noted between latitudes 55° and 44°, which we will call his 'northern nomenclature'. It turns out however, that the two nomenclatures actually overlap. The *Baia de los pinas* or 'bay of small ships' at 40°, also identified on Ortelius' revised world map, obviously represents the site of Drake's proposed colony, actually located 10 degrees to the north, on the east coast of Vancouver Island. Therefore, the second 'bay of small ships' near the bottom of the list must represent Drake's careenage, which is also noted in his northern nomenclature as the 'beautiful bay' at latitude 44°. It appears that 'beautiful young women' and 'bay of fires' respectively are additional descriptors used to differentiate between the two bays 'of small ships'. And so the intermediate places in this southern nomenclature are the highlights of his voyage between the secret colony site on Vancouver Island

The Northwest Coast of America on the 1589 maps of Hondius and Ortelius

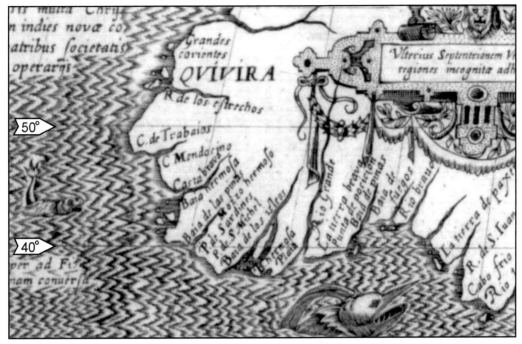

Hondius' *Americae*

Ortelius' *Maris Pacifici*

and his careenage. Thus, after 'beautiful young women' and two points of land, the name 'bay of islands' is placed at the mouth of a large, doubled channelled river which can only be the Fraser River, also identified in Ortelius' revised world map as a 'river of the straits' at 49°. Then, further down the coast is a 'great river', also identified in Ortelius' revised map of America, which could only be the mighty Columbia. It follows then, that the northern and southern nomenclatures not only dovetail but, together, confirm and compliment the information in Ortelius' revised maps of America and the world. Integration of the information in the three maps yields a remarkably rich description of the coast.[15]

Allowing for obvious redundancies it appears that there are nearly twenty distinct places described in this set of toponyms. Although there were some changes in the names applied to the particular capes, the three which are indicated, at 48°, 50° and 54°, match the latitudes of three of the most prominent capes on the entire northwest coast: Cape Flattery, Cape Cook and Cape Knox respectively. Notably the cape at 50°, which would be Cape Cook, corresponds to the first latitude written and covered over in the *Anonymous Narrative*, suggesting that this was Drake's initial landfall in the region. Then, the capes at 48° and 54° mark the openings to the Strait of Juan de Fuca and Dixon Entrance respectively, and reference to 'strong currents' at 54° and 55° gives further emphasis to the latter. It appears then that these were the openings by which Drake entered and exited the Inside Passage. Even more compelling are the three 'rivers of the straits' which are placed within one degree of the actual location of the three principal rivers of the Inside Passage: the Stikine (56° 40'), the Skeena (54°) and the Fraser (49°). Here then is confirmation that Drake must have sailed the length of the straits as indicated by the islands in the Dutch Drake map. Altogether, the information is entirely consistent with the picture which we have formed thus far.

It is particularly interesting that these toponyms were supplied to Ortelius in Spanish. Although Spanish was the language commonly associated with New World discovery, this certainly could not have been for the purpose of concealing Drake's discovery of these places from the Spanish, as they knew very well what places they had discovered and which ones they had not. Rather, it appears that the use of Spanish was designed to conceal from the English authorities the fact that the information had been leaked by an English source.

Information on Ortelius' Maps, 1587 - 1589

	Lat.	Toponym	Translation
	57½°	R. de los estrechos	river of the straits
	55°	Grandes Corrientes	strong currents
	54°	Grandes Corrientes	strong currents
	54°	Cab. Mendocino	cape Mendocino
	53°	R. de los estrechos	river of the straits
	50°	C. de Trabaios	cape of worries
x	50°	Baya de pinaz	bay of small ships
x	50°	Baia de los pinas,	bay of small ships
		also Mozzo hermosa	beautiful young women
*	—	P. de Sardines	point of small fish
*	—	P. St. Michel	point St. Michael
	49°	R. de los estrechos	river of the straits
*	49°	Baia de los isleos	bay of islands
*	—	B. hermosa	beautiful bay
	48°	C. de Trabaios	cape of worries
	48°	C. Mendocino	cape Mendocino
*	—	Plaia	beach
*	46°	Rio Grande	great river
*	46°	Rio Grande	great river
	46°	Costa brava	rugged coast
*	46°	La tierra brava	rugged land
*	—	Punta de pocicion	point of position
	44°	Baia hermosa	beautiful bay
*	44°	Baia de los Pinas,	bay of small ships
		also Baia de fuegos	bay of fires
	—	Rio Bravo	wild river

Drake's southern nomenclature:

x   indicates placement by adding back the 10° subtracted pursuant to the rule for relocating the secret colony site.

*   indicates placement as per the preceding discussion and by interpolation.

By 1589 Hondius was also involved in another cartographic project, which was the design and production of a pair of globes. In his introduction to *Principall Navigations* Hakluyt explains:

I have contented my selfe with inserting into the worke one of the best generall maps of the world only, untill the comming out of a very large and most exact terrestrial Globe collected and reformed according to the newest, secretest, and latest discoveries, both Spanish, Portugall, and English, composed by M. Emmerie Molyneux of Lambeth, a rare Gentleman in his profession, being therein for divers years, greatly supported by the purse and liberalite of the worshipfull marchant, M. William Sanderson.

Molyneux's terrestrial globe and its celestial mate were not only the first which would be produced in England, but also the largest undertaken anywhere up to this point.   One of London's most active merchant-adventurers, Sanderson had sponsored the three voyages of John Davis, in 1585, 1586 and 1587, in which he explored the strait which bears his name, running north between Greenland and Baffin Island. Davis had then introduced Molyneux to Sanderson. Undoubtedly the primary motivation behind the globe project was to illustrate as realistically as possible the relationship between Davis' discoveries and those of Drake, and the strategic potential of the northwest passage.   A mathematician, instrument-maker and collector of navigational information, Molyneux was assisted in the design of the globes by another mathematician, Edward Wright.[16]   And while Hondius has been credited only with engraving the globes, given his other involvements with Drake it is possible that he played a part in their design as well.

Further light may be shed on the early phase of this project by a pair of Dutch globes designed by Peter Plancius for Jacob van Langeren in 1589, because there appears to have been an exchange of information between the two projects.   On Plancius' celestial globe, the Southern Cross and the Southern Triangle are the same as on Molyneux's celestial globe, completed in 1592.[17]   On his terrestrial globe, however, Plancius introduced some new information in northwest America, and so the exchange appears to have occurred in or prior to 1589. It was not feasible to examine Plancius' globe in the present study, but in 1590 he published a double hemisphere map of the world (not shown) in which the toponyms are said to be the same as on the globe.[18]   In this Plancius' northwest coast, like that of Ortelius, is of the imaginary bulging type, and so again it appears that the information was supplied by latitude only. And again the toponyms are in Spanish:

Information on Plancius' Map, 1590

Lat.	Toponym	Translation
55°	C. Blanco	white cape
54°	Tierra Fisida (sic)	frozen land
51°	B. Hermosa	beautiful bay
50°	C. de fortuna	stormy cape
48°	C. de trabaios	cape of worries

While Plancius' information is rather limited in comparison to that given to Ortelius, this in itself is valuable because by its very brevity it appears that these are the principal highlights of Drake's explorations. Again two of the capes previously mentioned are noted, at 48° and 50°, except that the latter is now called *C. de fortuna*. Also he notes a 'beautiful bay' just above the 50th parallel, which presumably is synonymous with Drake's colony site. As *C. de* fortuna is inscribed at 50°, the bay has probably been displaced slightly to the north on the map. Then he notes 'frozen land' at about 54°, and so it appears that Drake encountered freezing weather in this latitude. And finally Plancius notes a 'white cape' at 55°, which suggests Cape Chacon at the southern tip of Prince of Wales Island, marking the entrance to Clarence Strait, which leads north between the island and the mainland and into the mouth of the Stikine River. Thus, Plancius' information too is consistent with the picture conveyed by the Dutch Drake map.

After Jodocus Hondius returned to the Netherlands, he published a world map known as the Christian Knight map, and in this his northwest coast of America contains exactly the same toponyms previously supplied to Plancius for inclusion on van Langeren's globe.[19] Then, after a lengthy legal fight over van Langeren's objections to his obtaining the necessary privilege from the Estates General, Hondius published his own *Globe of the earth revised and corrected in the year 1600*. The coastline on Hondius' globe is also imaginary, but the great bulge is eliminated and here he presents a new set of toponyms[20]:

Information on Hondius' globe, 1600

Lat.	Toponym	Translation
55°	C. de Fortuna	cape of good fortune
54°	Ancon de Ila	inlet of the island(s)
53°	Costa de los Tachaios	coast of objections
52°	Costa Brava	rugged coast
51°	Alcoanas	long inlet
50°	C. Mendocino	cape Mendocino
49°	Terra de Monthanus	mountainous land
48°	Cabo Nevada	cape of snowcapped mountains

Again there is the cape at 55°, as in Plancius' map. The word *fortuna* can mean either 'stormy' or 'good fortune'. In his map Plancius gives this name to the cape in 50°, which would be Cape Cook, and there the connotation certainly would be 'stormy'. But in the case of the cape at 55°, which would be Cape Chacon marking the entrance to northward-leading Clarence Strait, the connotation may well be 'good fortune'. *Ancon de Ila* or 'inlet of the island'—obviously 'island' should be plural—at 54° corresponds to Dixon Entrance. The name 'coast of objections' at 53° is especially intriguing and will be examined further at a later stage. The word *Alcoanas* is probably misspelled as there is no such word to be found in old Spanish, but it appears to be a derivative of the words *alcoba* for 'alcove' and *mas* for 'more', thus suggesting a continuous opening in the coast, and notably 51° is the latitude of Queen Charlotte Strait leading behind northern Vancouver Island. Then capes are again noted at 50° and 48°, the latter being aptly named 'cape of snowcapped mountains'.

Thus, in these works of Drake's cartographer Hondius, and of Ortelius and Plancius, we find a consistent and mutually corroborative picture of capes, straits and rivers in latitudes where Drake could be expected to discover such features based on our identification of the islands in the Dutch Drake map. It is important also that each cartographer's nomenclature contains toponyms which are not repeated in the other sets. Thereafter the information was copied, mixed and moved around in latitude by other cartographers in order to have something new to offer their clientele. But the maps examined here are the first where these toponyms appeared, and it is clear from the link to Drake in each instance that this is his information. Together then, they constitute an extremely valuable record of his otherwise secret explorations.

The Northwest Coast on the globe of Jodocus Hondius, 1600

Courtesy of the Huntington Library

It is especially interesting that Drake began disseminating this information, evidently with an understanding that it would not be published yet, in 1587, while in England his voyage was still tightly wrapped in official secrecy. In the information given to Ortelius the secret colony site is described as a 'bay of small ships' and placed at latitude 40°, so it appears that Drake was respecting the 10° rule governing its location on a map. From the numerous places identified above latitude 48° however, it appears that he wanted to be rid of the 48° cutoff rule. And with the publication of Hakluyt's remarkable map in Paris it appears that Walsingham too felt that the secrecy was excessive. But then with publication of the first map in England, the silver medallion map, it is clear that there the original coverup rules remained unchanged, and if anything, were strengthened insofar as the longitude of the coast was concerned. Thus, it appears that Drake had decided that leaking information to his contacts in the Dutch mapmaking community was the only means available to him for leaving clues to the true extent of his explorations.

CHAPTER FIVE

'That posterity be not deprived'

Philip's great invasion fleet finally appeared off the southwest coast of England in July 1588. After an eight day running fight the Spanish anchored off Calais, where the English sent fireships among them, and the following morning, scattered and in disarray, they took flight up the Channel into the North Sea. Soon afterward there began a succession of events which would slowly unravel Drake's commemorative project. On 4 September, Drake's powerful supporter Leicester suddenly collapsed and died. Then on 9 September Thomas Cavendish sailed triumphantly into Plymouth with a great load of plunder, having also circumnavigated the globe. Probably Drake had to wait until Cavendish reached London to hear the full story. From Plymouth Cavendish sent a dispatch to Walsingham:

> there be some things which I have kept from their [government officials'] sight for special causes which I mean to make known to your honour at my coming to London, for I protest before God that I will not hide any one thing from you, neither concerning the quantity of my goods nor *the secrets of the voyage, which in many things shall not be known but unto your honour for they be matters of great importance.*[1]　　　　　　(my italics)

Then the veil of official secrecy descended once again. A narrative of Cavendish's voyage by someone with the initials N.H. was included in Hakluyt's first edition of *Principall Navigations* in 1589, but it does not reveal anything about the northern venture. However, a revised account which was attributed to one Francis Pretty and substituted in Hakluyt's second edition a decade later provides a glimpse of what had transpired.[2] Cavendish entered Magellan's Strait in January 1587, and after stopping to inspect the abandoned Spanish fortifications emerged into the Pacific 49 days later. By September they were off the coast of Baja California having sunk 19 ships and burned Acapulco. There they lay in wait at Cape San Lucas for the Manila galleon making its annual return from the Philippines, and on 4 November they captured the richly laden *Santa Ana*. After putting her occupants ashore Cavendish plundered and burned the galleon and then set sail across the Pacific, making his first landfall in the Marianas 42 days later. After a brief sojourn in the Philippines he set his course for home via the Cape of Good Hope. Notably, he showed no interest in the Moluccas, and the voyage from Mexico to England took less than 10 months, in contrast to Drake's 17 months.

According to Francis Pretty however, Cavendish's second ship, the *Content,* did not accompany them when they departed Cape San Lucas, and they never saw her again. Then he tells of an incident which occurred in the Philippines. Cavendish had brought with him one of the Spanish pilots, a man named Ersola. When they reached the Philippines, Ersola was caught trying to smuggle a letter via the islanders to Manila. Pretty says the letter told of Cavendish's raids and, "he farther signified, that wee were ... but one shippe ... and that the other ship, as he supposed, was *gone for the North-west passage, standing in 55 degrees"* [3] (my italics). The words 'as he supposed' would leave some room for doubt but for the fact that a printed note in the margin of Hakluyt's page calls attention to "the Northwest passage". It appears that Ersola had somehow obtained some vital information about Drake's Strait of Anian, and evidently discovery of his letter sealed his fate. Pretty says that Cavendish promptly hanged him.

From Cape San Lucas in November, the *Content* would have been expected to get through the passage the following summer and reach England by the time Cavendish returned, but it had not. Moreover, Cavendish now reported that he had seen nothing to support Drake's claim that the extremity of South America was comprised of islands.[4] The inference is obvious: if that discovery was a figment of Drake's imagination, then his claim to have discovered the Strait of Anian might also be. Drake must have been furious. Despite the disappointment and Cavendish's doubts however, Drake's commemorative project now got the go ahead, although this appears to have been principally Walsingham's doing. Toward Christmas Michael Mercator was commissioned to engrave the silver medallion map of Drake's voyage, and in Paris Hakluyt began packing to return to London. Hakluyt had for some time been assembling material for his ambitious new work, *The Principall Navigations, Voiages and Discoveries of the English nation,* but this of course would be manifestly incomplete without an account of the greatest voyage of all. The book would be printed under Walsingham's authority by the Queen's printer's deputies, George Bishop and Ralph Newberie, and so it appears that Walsingham placed considerable importance on its propaganda value.[5] By mid 1589 they had begun printing the first parts, including Hakluyt's title page promising an account of a voyage to "*Nova Albion,* vpon the backside of *Canada*".

Meanwhile the conflict with Spain entered a new phase. Drake's instructions, issued in February 1589, called for an ambitious campaign of retribution against King Philip. He was to destroy the still largely intact Armada, now repairing in northern Spain, and then support an army under Sir John Norris in the occupation of Lisbon and installation of the pretender Don Antonio on the throne of Portugal. Drake sailed in mid April with a force of 13,000 soldiers and 4,000 seamen in 180 ships. But the English armada proved unwieldy and the expedition failed to achieve any of its objectives. In October Drake and Norris were brought before a board of inquiry to answer for their conduct, but both gave reasonable explanations for their actions and the matter was dropped. Within a year Norris was back at the head of an army. Soon afterward however, Drake retired to the West Country and nearly three years would pass before he became active at court again. Then sometime around the end of November, with *The Principall Navigations* awaiting binding, Hakluyt was obliged to add a note to the reader offering an excuse for not including his promised account of Drake's voyage around the world:

> I must confesse to haue taken more then ordinarie paines, *meaning to haue inserted it* in this worke: but being of late (contrary to my expectation) seriously delt withall, not to anticipate or preuent another mans paines and charge in drawing all the seruices of that worthie Knight into one volume I haue yeelded vnto those of my friendes which pressed me in the matter, referring the further knowledge of his proceedings, to those intended discourses.
> (my italics)

The most vivid and detailed account of Drake's voyage is *The World Encompassed by Sir Francis Drake*, published by his nephew and namesake in 1628. The title page explains that the account, "offered now at last to publique view", was "carefully collected out of the notes of Master Francis Fletcher Preacher in this imployment, and divers others his [Drake's] followers in the same [voyage]". Professor David B. Quinn, a leading authority on the writings of Richard Hakluyt, argues convincingly that part of Hakluyt's "The Famous Voyage" as eventually published was adapted from a draft of *The World Encompassed* which was written for Drake by Philip Nichols.[6] Nichols sailed with Drake as chaplain and secretary on his 1585 Caribbean expedition and again on his 1587 Cadiz raid, and probably continued in his service for some years. He first wrote *Sir Francis Drake Revived*, recounting Drake's early exploits in the Caribbean, which was finally published by Drake's nephew in 1626. Then, it appears, he wrote a draft of *The World Encompassed*, subtitled as "being the next voyage to that to Nombre de Dios", to which Drake subsequently made some revisions.[7] In all probability then, Hakluyt's excuse that he was "seriously delt withall, not to anticipate or preuent another mans paines" refers to Nichols' intended account of the voyage.

Here however, it is necessary to consider whether Hakluyt's excuse is legitimate. As Quinn points out, only part of Hakluyt's account as eventually published was adapted from Nichols' draft of *The World Encompassed*—namely, Drake's northern voyage (plus, perhaps, a few embellishments elsewhere in his journey). As previously noted, the remainder of Hakluyt's account of the voyage from the Strait of Magellan onward is adapted from the *Anonymous Narrative*. And that narrative included an account, albeit heavily abridged, of Drake's northern voyage. Then at some point his adaptation from Nichols' draft was substituted for it. It therefore appears that Hakluyt had to have been in possession of an account of the voyage, the initial draft of which was the *Anonymous Narrative*, before Nichols' produced his draft account, and so Hakluyt's excuse for not including Drake's voyage in his newly printed book was a fabrication. Most probably this earlier account was the one prepared for Henry of Navarre and also sent to Prince Wilhelm of Hesse, which Hakluyt himself had possibly written working from a now-lost journal that Walsingham had given him in 1585. Then in 1589, in keeping with Walsingham's desire to aggressively propagandize England's claims in North America and the Pacific, a decision evidently was taken to place more emphasis on Drake's northern voyage and Nova Albion, and Nichols' adaptation from Fletcher's journal was the best material available for the purpose.

The sanctimonious preacher Fletcher was critical of Drake's conduct on the voyage, and it has been suggested that Drake confiscated his journal when they reached England in order to suppress its contents.[8] But given the standing order, first seen with Frobisher's voyages, that all such material was to be gathered and handed over to the crown immediately, it would hardly have been politic for Drake to admit to possession of Fletcher's journal at this late date. It is most likely that Fletcher's journal was one of several turned over in 1580 to Walsingham, who had the job of responding to various Spanish charges against Drake, and that Drake had retrieved it from him sometime since. There is a surviving manuscript account of the voyage from England to the island of Mocha in Chile which was written in 1677 and which the writer, a London apothecary named Conyers, states was a faithful copy of Fletcher's journal, which was loaned to him.[9] However, Conyers' copy contains a rebuttal of Cavendish's doubt that Tierra del Fuego was an archipelago,[10] which could not have been written before his return in 1588, and given the animosity between Fletcher and Drake it is highly unlikely that Fletcher would have resurfaced in 1588 to defend Drake's reputation in any matter. In all probability then, this was Drake's own rebuttal of Cavendish, added to Fletcher's narrative by Nichols sometime in the fall of that year as he began adapting Drake's account from it. Then, Quinn explains, Hakluyt probably obtained Nichols' initial draft from Drake sometime in the spring of 1589. Quinn concludes that the most likely reason for Hakluyt's inability to publish the account was Drake's apparent fall from favour as a consequence of the Lisbon debacle.[11] However, there may have been more than this behind the matter.

In Hakluyt's note to the reader he uses the words 'meaning to have inserted it', and notably the account was not integrated with the pagination of the volume. Instead, the last word on page 643 and the first word on page 644, between which the account was eventually inserted, is "instructions". Yet the title page to Hakluyt's book, printed a few months previous, unequivocally promises that an account of the voyage will be provided. It appears then that some uncertainty must have arisen in the interval. So what was the reason for the uncertainty? One possible reason, as Quinn suggests, is that Elizabeth, angered by Drake's failure to fulfil the objectives of the Lisbon expedition, ordered Walsingham to put his commemorative project on hold. Also however, it seems clear that the mission of Cavendish's other ship had been to complete the discovery of the northwest passage, and it appears most likely that this was the reason Drake's commemorative project had been held in abeyance to this point. Then Cavendish had returned reporting that the Spanish had somehow obtained vital information of Drake's strait. No doubt there had been hope that the *Content* with its load of treasure would return the following summer when the ice again cleared from the passage, or via the Cape of Good Hope as Drake had done. But by the fall of 1589 it was obvious that she would not return. Therefore, the question of what, if anything, should be published about Drake's northern reconnaissance may have proven more contentious with Elizabeth and the Privy Council than Walsingham had anticipated.

Then Drake may have exacerbated the problem by proposing that he now lead a new expedition to the Pacific. Certainly it would have been in character for him to do so after Cavendish questioned the reliability of his discoveries, and of course he had advocated taking the war to Philip's Pacific colonies many times. Indeed, Elizabeth may well have held out that he would finally be allowed to go once he had conclusively disposed of the Spanish invasion fleet. But his recent expedition had failed to do so, and the suggestion that he now be allowed to go off to the Pacific would likely have infuriated her.

Exactly when Hakluyt *was* allowed to distribute "The Famous Voyage" to his readers has never been determined. Quinn suggests that he inserted it in all but a few copies of *Principall Navigations* sometime in the early months of 1590, before they were distributed.[12] However, Drake biographer Harry Kelsey points out that contemporary historian John Stow, in his 1592 *Chronicles,* was able to draw from Hakluyt's account of Cavendish's voyage in *Principall Navigations*, but seemingly not from his account of Drake's voyage. Kelsey therefore argues that the socalled 'Drake leaves' could not have been distributed by Hakluyt until sometime after that date.[13] There are two additional reasons for considering this possibility. First, Walsingham, who had been in poor health, died on 6 April 1590. Thus, Drake's last powerful champion was taken from Elizabeth's council, and the question of commemorating his voyage was left in less aggressive hands. And secondly, it appears that plans were soon afoot for yet another attempt to complete the discovery of the passage. Cavendish's instructions were not finally issued until the end of June 1591, but it is obvious from the scale of the expedition that the preparations had been underway for many months. This time Cavendish was to take five ships, including the bark *Desire* under the command of veteran arctic explorer John Davis. Cavendish was to escort Davis to the Californias, and undoubtedly from there Davis

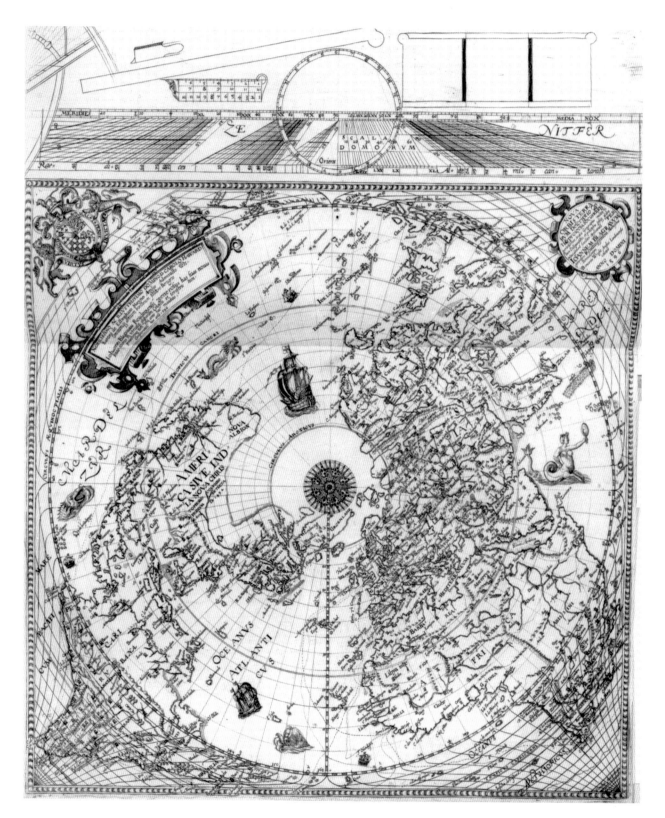

The Blagrave map, 1596

was to continue north with the aim of finding the connection to his strait. The expedition sailed on 25 August 1591.

That same month, before Cavendish and Davis sailed, Emery Molyneux presented his much anticipated terrestrial globe to Elizabeth at Greenwich, where it was later seen "covered by a taffeta curtain in the form of a dome encompassing it down to the ground".[14] Molyneux's plan was to produce more of the globes for distribution to persons of importance in England and abroad. Evidently however, the globe which Hakluyt had heralded as containing 'the newest, secretest and latest discoveries' was deemed appropriate for viewing only by a selected audience. Sometime later, Molyneux's sponsor William Sanderson hosted a lavish entertainment at his home where he presented another terrestrial globe to Elizabeth,[15] and it appears that this edition was intended for wider viewing. There is a surviving Molyneux globe which was once owned by Sir Walter Raleigh, and which is dated 1592 and inscribed "Author, Iodicus Hondius". However, Hondius later stated that he engraved yet another globe in 1593.[16] Unfortunately, the surface of Raleigh's globe (not shown) is badly damaged in the region of the North Pacific. What can be made out, however, is a westward bulging North American coastline similar to that of Ortelius. Nova Albion is no longer visible on the globe, but a contemporary scholar records that it was inscribed at latitude 46°.[17] Most intriguingly however, when some restoration work was being done on the globe in 1951, fragments of a different globe map were found under the surface,[18] and when further restoration was done recently it was confirmed that this underlying layer contained the gores for another globe.[19] The suggestion then is that Raleigh's globe was a third edition, engraved by Hondius in 1593 but retaining the date 1592, and may simply have been pasted over a globe previously displaying the second edition.

In 1596, the year Drake died, mathematician John Blagrave published a book titled *Astrolabium Uranicum Generale*, "whereunder for their [the readers'] delight he hath annexed another inuention, expressing in one face the whole Globe terrestrial; with the two great english voyages lately performed around the world". Blagrave's map, a remarkable polar projection, is based on a Molyneux globe, but a different one from that owned by Raleigh. From England, dotted lines trace the routes of Drake and Cavendish around South America, in the lower left corner, and then northward in the Pacific. Drake's track turns back at latitude 48°, where the coastline is placed 155° west of England—some 30° closer than on Raleigh's globe. Where Drake's track reverses there is a notch in the coast, and *Nova Albion* is inscribed nearby. Then at latitude 60° an English ship is depicted emerging from the northwest passage into the Pacific after a short voyage from England, in sharp contrast to the long journey Drake and Cavendish had to take around South America and then homeward around Asia and Africa. Here then is the vision of the passage in all its splendour. Notably however, none of the three surviving copies of

Blagrave's map was found with his book. It appears that the map, like the globe on which it was based, was suppressed.

Sometime prior to June 1597 Molyneux emigrated to Amsterdam, taking with him the copper plates for the globe which is illustrated in Blagrave's map.[20] In Amsterdam a few minor additions were made to the plates and Molyneux produced another globe.[21] Then following his death in 1599 the date of the globe was altered, it appears by pen, from 1592 to 1603—the year of Elizabeth's death—and it and a celestial mate still dated 1592 were acquired by William Crashaw, preacher at Drake's favourite institution, the Middle Temple, London.[22] On the terrestrial globe the coastlines are positioned exactly as in Blagrave's map, and the details match those on the fragments of gores found under the surface of Raleigh's globe.[23]

On the northwest coast of America, a *B. de pinas* is placed at latitude 40°, as in the information given to Ortelius, but Drake's track, now only faintly visible, continues northward without stopping there. At 48° it turns back as per the original coverup rule, and returns southward to a *C. Mendocino* at 43° before heading off across the Pacific. From *C. Mendocino*, a boundary line follows a river inland, recalling the boundaries in the Drake Mellon map and the French Drake map. Most interesting of all however, at 48° the coast turns sharply eastward into a large indentation which unmistakably matches the shape of the mainland coast behind Vancouver Island. Plainly the distinctive configuration of this hidden inner coastline could not have been depicted with such accuracy unless Drake had sailed the length of the straits separating the island from it.[24] Adjacent to the missing island, *Nova Albion* is inscribed straddling the 50th parallel, and below that, *F. Dracus*. There can be little doubt then that the 1591 globe which Elizabeth kept under the curtain at Greenwich depicted the island of Nova Albion, and probably the Queen Charlottes and Prince of Wales Island as well. Then notwithstanding removal of the islands, it appears that the longitude and configuration of the coastline and the inscription of *Nova Albion* at 50° which this globe retained was deemed still too revealing, and Hondius was obliged to engrave the third edition depicting the bulging continent as found on Raleigh's globe. We return then to 1592, when Molyneux's suppressed globe was originally produced.

By April 1592 Cavendish and Davis had made it partway through Magellan's Strait, but found that they could make no further headway due to contrary winds, after which they became separated. Cavendish fell ill and died at sea in June, and his men turned back for England. Davis made three more attempts and on the third reached the Pacific, but then with his sails in tatters and threatened with mutiny he was obliged to turn back as well. He finally reached the coast of Ireland in June 1593 with only 15 men out of his original company of 76 remaining. Cavendish's ship had already returned in late 1592 with the news of his death and the

Molyneux's suppressed 1592 globe reissued in Amsterdam in 1603

Photograph by Roy Fox

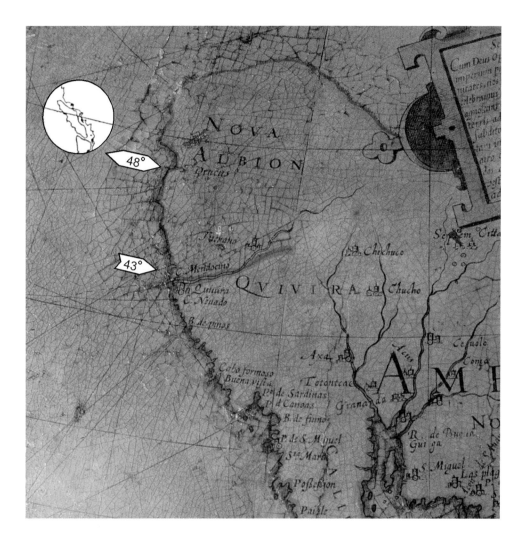

Nova Albion on Molyneux's suppressed globe
Photograph by Roy Fox

This and the photograph on the preceding page
by the kind permission of the Masters of the Bench of the
Honourable Society of the Middle Temple

disappearance of Davis. Sometime in this same year, as previously noted, John Stow published his account of Drake's voyage in his *Chronicles*. His account of the northern voyage is brief:

> the 16 of March being on land at the Ile of Canoes [Costa Rica], he passed foorth northward till he came to the *latitude of forty seauen, thinking to have come that way home*; but being constrained by fogs and cold winds to foresake his purpose, came backeward to the lineward the tenth of June 1579, and stayed in the *latitude of thirty eight* to graue and trim his ship, untill the five and twenty of July, and from thence setting his course Southwest.[25]
>
> (my italics)

As Kelsey points out, some of Stow's particulars are different from those in Hakluyt's "The Famous Voyage". The latitude of 47° which Stow gives for Drake's northern reach and the date of 10 June are not found anywhere else. However, the first and last dates which Stow cites are found in *The World Encompassed*, and one other detail clearly links his account to Hakluyt. As in "The Famous Voyage" as eventually published, Stow has the sequence of the voyage mixed up so that Drake is described as setting sail for northwest America from the island of Cano in Costa Rica, rather than from Guatulco. Very possibly then, Stow's account is a glimpse of the still-unpublished narrative which Hakluyt had adapted, in this respect erroneously, from Nichols' draft account. Hakluyt and Stow were in the habit of exchanging such material. It appears that sometime in 1592 a decision was taken to finally allow publication of the story of Drake's voyage, and Stow's brief account was approved while Hakluyt's longer version was still under review. Conceivably the latitude of 47° which Stow gives for Drake's northern reach was derived by the official censor subtracting 10° from his true reach of 57°.[26] But then it appears there were more deliberations on the question of what was to be said about Drake's northern voyage.

By Christmas 1592 Drake was active again at court. It appears that Elizabeth's treasury was running low, as soon thereafter there would be discussion of him leading a new expedition to the Caribbean. Then on 1 January 1593 Drake wrote to her [27]:

> Madam,
> Seeing divers [others] have diversly reported and written of these voyages and actions which I have attempted and made, every one endeavouring to bring to light whatsoever inklings of conjectures they have had; *whereby many untruths have been published, and the certain truth concealed, as I have thought it necessary myself* ... so I have accounted it to present this discourse to Your Majesty ... being the first fruits of thy servant's pen *that posterity be not deprived* of such help as may happily be gained thereby [28]
>
> (my italics)

Drake added that he hoped his labour "in writing the report thereof" would not be wasted. His reference to 'these voyages' indicates that he was also submitting *Sir Francis Drake Revived*, but it is obvious that the words 'the certain truth concealed, as I have thought it necessary myself' and his appeal 'that posterity be not deprived' relate to *The World Encompassed*. Thus, Drake was now presenting his own edited version of Nichols' draft for Elizabeth's approval. Evidently permission for its publication was withheld however, and it is not hard to discern what was found objectionable about it. Explaining the purpose of the northern voyage, the account states:

> considering ... that the time of the yeare now drew on wherein we must attempt, or of necessitie wholly give ouer that action, which chiefly our Generall had determined, namely, the discouery of what passage there was to found about the Northerne parts of America, from the South Sea, into our owne Ocean ... which could not at all be done if the opportunity of time were now neglected, we therefore all of us [agreed] ... to hasten on our intended iourney for the discouery of the said passage.

Then the voyage is described as follows:

> From Guatulco we departed the day following, viz April 16, setting our course directly into the sea, whereon we sayled 500 leagues in longitude to get a winde: and betweene that and June 3, 1400 leagues in all [4,200 miles], till we came into 42 deg. of North latitude, where in the night following we found such alteration of heate, into extreame and nipping cold, that our men in generall did grieuously complaine thereof ... [and] the day following ... the raine which fell was an vnnatural and frozen substance, so that we seemed rather to be in the frozen Zone ...

> Neither did this happen for the time onely ... for it came to that extremity in sayling but 2 deg. farther to the Northward in our course that ... our meate as soone as it was remooued from the fire, would presently in a manner be frozen vp, and our ropes and tackling in a few dayes were growne to that stiffnesse, that what 3 men afore were able with them to performe, now 6 men ... were hardly able to accomplish: whereby a sudden and great discouragement seased vpon the mindes of our men ... yet would not our general be discouraged, but as wel by confortable speeches ... as also by other good and profitable perswasions ... so stirred them vp ... to indure some short extremity to haue the speedier comfort, and a little trouble to obtaine the greater glory ...

The 5 day of Iune, wee were forced by contrary windes to runne in with the shoare, which we then first descried, and to cast anchor in a bad bay ... where wee were not without some danger by reason of the many extreme gusts and flawes that beate upon vs ...

From the height of 48 deg., in which now we were to 38, we found the land, by coasting alongst it ... being couered with snow.

In 38 deg. 30 min. we fell in with a conuenient and fit harborough, and Iune 17 came to anchor therein: where we continued till the 23 day of Iuly following.

The narrative then returns to the subject of the freezing weather, describing some Indians who "come shiuering to vs in their warme furres, crowding close together, body to body, to recieve heat of one another", and discussing the causes. Altogether, nearly 1,000 words are devoted to the extreme weather they encountered and then, regarding the outcome of the search for the passage the account states:

And also from these reasons we coniecture, that either there is no passage at all through these Northerne coasts (which is most likely), or if there be, that it be vnnauigable. Adde hereunto, that though we searched the coast diligently, euen vnto the 48 deg., yet found we not the land to trend so much as one point in any place toward the East, but rather running on continually North-west, as if it went directly to meet with Asia, and euen in that height ... yet we had a smooth and calme sea, with ordinary flowing and reflowing, which could not haue been had there been a frete [strait], of which we rather infallibly concluded ... that there was none.

The narrative then returns to the anchorage, where it describes the Indians as going *mostly naked*, their 'crowning' of Drake, his act of possession, and his naming of the surrounding country Nova Albion.[29] In "The Famous Voyage" on the other hand, Hakluyt describes the northern voyage as follows:

Our Generall ... began to consider and to consult of the best way for his Countrey.

He thought it not good to returne by the Streightes [of Magellan], for two speciall causes ... he resolued therefore to auoide these hazards, to goe forward to the Islands of the Moluccass, and therehence to saile the course of the Portingals by the Cape of Bona Sperenza.

Upon this resolution, he began to thinke of his best way to the Moluccas, and finding himselfe where he nowe was becalmed, he sawe, that of necessitie he must be forced to take a Spanish course, namely to saile somewhat Northerly to get a wind. We therefore set saile, and sailed in longitude 600. leagues at the least for a good winde, and thus much we sailed from the 16. of Aprill, till the 3. of June

The 5. day of June, being in 42. degrees towards the pole Arctike, we found the aire so colde, that our men being greeuiously pinched with the same, complained of the extremitie thereof, and the further we went, the more the cold increased vpon vs. Whereupon we thought it best for that time to seeke the land, and did so, finding it not mountainous, but lowe plaine land, & clad, and couered ouer with snowe, so that we drewe backe againe without landing, till we came within 38. degrees toward the line. In which heigth it pleased God to send vs into a faire and good Baye, with a good winde to enter the same.

After just these few words concerning the voyage, Hakluyt turns to events at the anchorage. This portion of his narrative, as Quinn points out, is simply an abridged adaptation of *The World Encompassed*. Apparently then, notwithstanding Nichols' and Drake's extensive editing of Fletcher's journal to conform to the 48° cutoff, and the denial that he had found the Strait of Anian, the admission that he had gone in search of it and his long discussion of the freezing weather, implying a higher latitude exploration, revealed too much. Consequently the account was suppressed and Hakluyt was instructed to remove the offending references from his adaptation of it. Ultimately, he portrays Drake as setting off for the Moluccas but then being blown back onto the coast of America, where he repairs his ship and, finding the Indians friendly, decides to take them under Elizabeth's protection. In the process of revision however, Hakluyt inadvertently retained one detail from his earlier draft, as it is subsequently eliminated in his second edition: in the adjacent margin a printed note states "A purpose in Sir Francis to returne by the Northwest Passage". Most probably then, Stow's account *was* based on an earlier draft of "The Famous Voyage".

Especially noteworthy however, although Stow says that Drake repaired his ship at 38°, he does not mention Nova Albion. Evidently at the time of his writing Drake's stopping place and Nova Albion were still being treated as separate places, as on the Silver Medallion map and Molyneux's globe. It therefore appears that up to this point both "The Famous Voyage" and Nichols' draft account continued to place Nova Albion "vpon the backside of *Canada*" while asserting that Drake did not land until he reached his careenage. Most probably the latitude of 38° which Stow gives for the careenage was derived from the cryptogram in the maps indicating the mouth of the inlet in that latitude. In other words the maps, having been produced beforehand, became the principal reference point in the deliberations about what was to be said in the written accounts. And eventually the result was a decision that in both the maps and the accounts Nova Albion had to be consolidated with the fictitious stopping place. But what would explain the difference in latitude—38° versus 38° 30'—given by Hakluyt and Drake respectively for Nova Albion? Again the inlet cryptogram appears to have been the key point of reference. Most probably Drake had proposed 38° 30' because in the strict meaning of the cryptogram this would place Nova Albion where it belongs, on the 'peninsula' above the mouth of the inlet.

Now we come at last to the splendid Broadside map of Jodocus Hondius. Clearly this is the ultimate design of Drake's commemorative map, no doubt a product of years of effort during which there must have been several drafts, as with Molyneux's globe and the written accounts. Notably, the information of Cavendish's first voyage has been added after the original conception of the map. In contrast to Drake's route, which is embellished with the now familiar scheme of little ships, nowhere is Cavendish's progress marked by his three ships. Elsewhere, the texts in the main legend and the one at the lower right, and the addition of the note below Tierra del Fuego are the only other references to Cavendish. Imagine the removal of these, and it becomes obvious that the original purpose of the map was solely to commemorate Drake's voyage. All of the scenes decorating its borders memorialize his exploits. In the lower corners of the map are the same ones previously depicted in Drake's private maps. Below the hemispheres is the *Golden Hinde* in profile, and in the upper corners are views of two additional stopping points on the voyage: on the right is the port of Tjilatjap in Java, and on the left *Portus Nova Albionis*. The latter depicts a ship and a fortified encampment, indicating that this is the harbour in northwest America where Drake careened his ship. In this the Indians are shown gathered around the bay lighting fires, which is a scene described only in *The World Encompassed*, on the occasion of Drake's departure from there.

Notably also, the Queen's coat of arms and portrait surmount the world at the junction of its hemispheres. Inclusion of her portrait recalls Samuel Purchas' description of "the Map of Sir Francis Drakes Voyage presented to Queen Elizabeth, still hanging in His Majesties Gallerie at White Hall", and so there is reason to suspect that the map which Purchas describes was actually a deluxe first edition of this map, presented to her much as the first Molyneux globe was. If so, it very likely depicted the configuration of Northwest America much more realistically. Then however, Hondius was no doubt obliged to fatten North America as in the case of Molyneux's third globe, as it now projects in longitude some 200° west of England. Probably this also was when he was required to incorporate Cavendish's voyage in

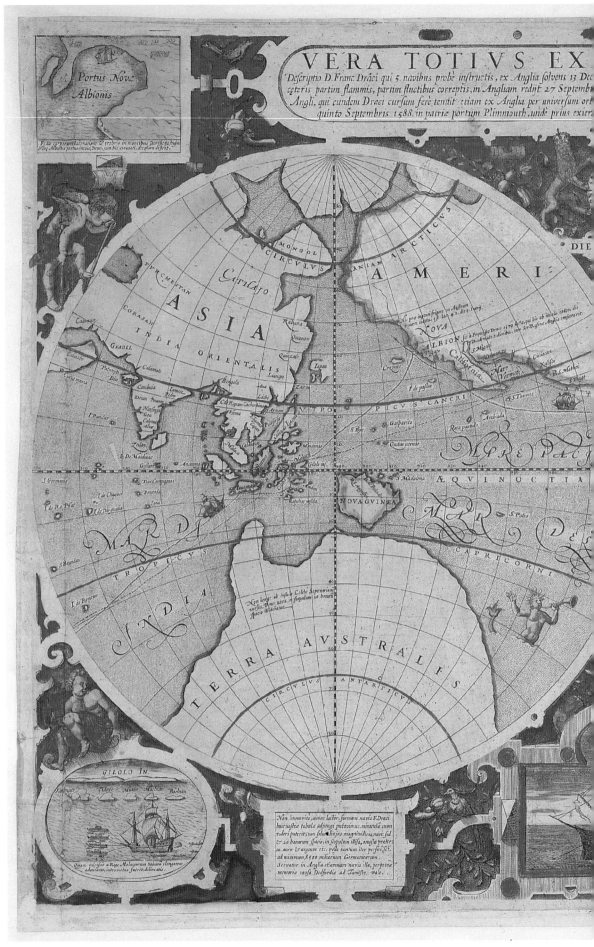

The Broadside map by Jodocus Hondius, circa 1593 – 1595
Printed and hand-coloured

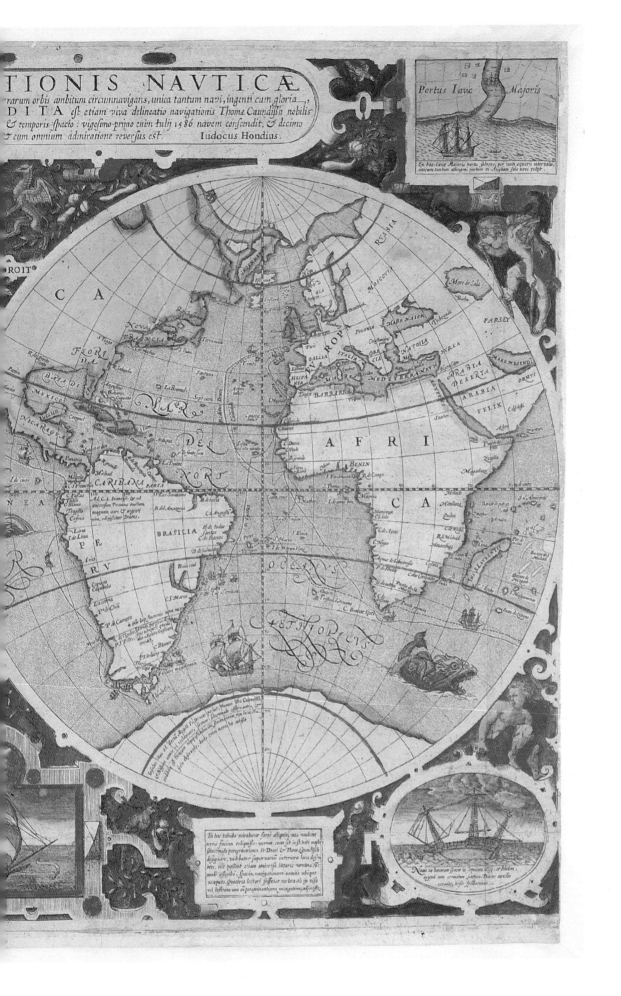

TIONIS NAVTICAE

rarum orbis ambitum circunnavigans, unica tantum navi, ingenti cum gloria,
DITA est etiam viva delineatio navigationis Thomæ Caundiſsh nobilis
& temporis ſpacio: vigeſino-primo enim Iulij 1586 navem conſcendit, & decimo
cum omnium admiratione reverſus est.   Iudocus Hondius.

Portus Iavæ   Majoris

Ex hac Iavæ Majoris portu ſolvens, per tanti æquoris interualia,
unicum tantum attingens; jortum et Angliam ſola navi rediit.

C   A

RUSSIA

GROENLAND

ROIT

NOVA
FRANCIA

FLORI
DA

MAR

EVROPA

Moscovi

MARE MAIOR

POLONIA

GALLIA   ITALIA
HISPA
NIA   MARE
Tanga BARBARIA   MEDITERRANEVM

FARSEY

ARABIA
DESERTA

ARABIA
FELIX

ORMVS

AFRI

DEL

BENIN

CA

MEXICO

NICARAG

CARIBANA

NORT

BRASILIA

PE

RV

OCEANVS

ÆTHIOPICVS

C. Bonæ ſpei

Nova Albion on the Broadside map

the map. It certainly seems unlikely that Drake would have volunteered to do so. And finally, on the finished plate Hondius has been obliged to erase Drake's track southward from 48° to about 42°, where an asterisk corresponds to an inscription, still at 48°, explaining that Drake turned back here because of the cold (the erased track is still faintly visible). Again the inlet scheme is used to depict Drake's stopping place, but now *Nova Albion* is inscribed straddling the 40th parallel instead of the 50th parallel as on Molyneux's suppressed globe, or at 48° as on the silver medallion map. But there is another, more subtle change from the silver medallion which is especially interesting. Drake's track now runs northward past the 'peninsula', and then reappears emerging southbound from the inlet behind it, indicating that he sailed out of the Strait of Juan de Fuca on his return southward, rather than into it on his way northward.

Most important however, is that before Drake's track was erased southward from 48° the map conformed to *The World Encompassed*, and after his track was erased back to 42°, the map conformed to "The Famous Voyage". Thus, Hondius' map uniquely captures the rejection of Drake's account in favour of the official account rendered by Hakluyt. And allowing that the map obviously was intended to accompany *The World Encompassed*, which was not submitted to Elizabeth until January 1593, it appears that Hondius was required to make this last change sometime that year, because before the end of 1593 he emigrated back to the Netherlands. Indeed, with both Drake's map and Molyneux's globe finally completed after years of effort, Hondius probably had had his fill of working under official scrutiny. As three of the surviving copies of his map were found in English books, it appears that it was issued in England prior to his relocating to the Netherlands. Most probably then, Hakluyt's 'Drake leaves' also were finally released sometime in the latter part of 1593.[30] Then in 1595 Hondius reissued the map in Amsterdam, where it was pasted on a broadsheet containing accounts of Drake's and Cavendish's voyages; hence the term 'Broadside' map. The accounts are adapted from Hakluyt except for one detail: where Hakluyt states that Drake named "this countrey" Nova Albion, the broadsheet states that he named "this Island" Nova Albion.[31] It appears that Hondius could not resist correcting the official account on this one crucial point.

CHAPTER SIX

The Last Glimpses

In June 1593 Richard Hawkins, the only son of Drake's kinsman John Hawkins, set sail from Plymouth at the head of a new expedition for the Pacific. Curiously, although Hawkins later said that he did so "with the Council's consent", it appears that he sailed without a commission from Elizabeth.[1] He would later write that his voyage was intended for the islands of Japan, the Moluccas, the Kingdom of China and the East Indies. Following his capture by the Spanish, however, he admitted that he was bound for the Californias. There is also a hint that some great enterprise was to be launched as soon as he returned to England.[2] Hawkins managed to get through Magellan's Strait, but the Spanish had now installed a fleet of swift, well-armed frigates to patrol the coast from Valparaiso to Panama. South of Callao he narrowly escaped six of them, but then they trapped him in the Bay of Atacames and after three days of fighting which left himself and most of his men wounded, he surrendered. While imprisoned Hawkins learned of the deaths of both his father and Drake from illness at sea in the Caribbean.

After Drake's death in 1596 the quest for the northwest passage via the South Sea came to an end. When he recovered from his ordeal, John Davis published *Worlde's Hydrographical Description* in which he argued that the northwest passage truly existed and urged that it should be a matter of the greatest interest to England, but all of the influential men who had backed Drake's plan were now dead and Elizabeth was no doubt weary of the subject. It appears however, that someone among her officials believed that the project might one day be resurrected, because the cloak of secrecy continued and a further effort was made to amend Hakluyt's account of Drake's northern voyage. The result, however, was more inconsistencies.

In his second edition of *Principall Navigations* (1600), Hakluyt presented two accounts of the voyage. First he revised "The Famous Voyage", removing the reference to sailing 'in longitude' and to the northern coast being covered in snow, as well as the note in the margin referring to Drake's intended return via the northwest passage. Also, for some obscure reason he altered Drake's northern reach from 42° to 43° while retaining the sailing distance from Guatulco as "600 leagues at the least". Then he included in the same volume a second account devoted exclusively to Drake's northern voyage.[3] In this he repeats the latitude of 43° but gives Drake's sailing distance as "800 leagues at the least". Also, he introduces the date of 17 June for Drake's arrival at his anchorage, as in *The World Encompassed*. Undoubtedly the main purpose of this additional account was to emphasize

England's claim of sovereignty over the region. Thus, she was poised to resume her efforts to discover the passage and occupy Nova Albion at some future date.

In all events, one or another version of Hakluyt's narrative served as the basis for all of the published accounts of Drake's northern exploit until *The World Encompassed* was "offered now at last to publique view" in 1628, by which time few of Drake's contemporaries remained to add anything to the record. However, two who survived beyond that date did put to paper some additional information.

In 1573 the Earl of Leicester secretly married the widowed Lady Sheffield, and the following year she bore him a son, who was given his father's name, Robert Dudley. But when Elizabeth learned of the secret union she was enraged and refused to accept the legitimacy of either the marriage or the infant as Leicester's heir. The younger Robert was eventually accepted at court however, and there he met Thomas Cavendish, recently returned from his voyage around the world. Then in 1591 he married Cavendish's sister Anne, and following Cavendish's death served as executor of his estate. Coming into possession of two of Cavendish's ships, Dudley proposed to lead a new expedition to the Pacific, but was dissuaded, probably by Drake, and sailed instead to the West Indies in 1594. After Leicester's death Dudley petitioned the court for recognition that he was his father's rightful heir, but was unsuccessful and in 1605 he emigrated to Italy, where he spent the remainder of his life. Around 1630 he began work on an atlas of charts, which was eventually published in 1647, after his death.

Dudley's atlas, beautifully engraved in Florence and titled *Arcano del Mare*, contains two charts depicting the Pacific coast of North America. They are based on a set of manuscript drawings which have been preserved in the State Library of Bavaria since the 18th century. These are not seacharts, but rather rough drawings in which Dudley appears to have been contemplating where to place some features copied from another source. The one finished drawing which was not published depicts a coastline which includes a *B. di nova Albion* at latitude 38° and an inscription explaining that it was discovered by *Draco Inglese* in 1579. In the bay, which bears a vague resemblance to the drawing labelled *Portus Nova Albionis* in the corner of Hondius' Broadside map, Dudley shows an anchor and some soundings in fathoms, which indicate that it is a fairly shallow bay. In the scale of the chart however, the mouth of the bay is about eight miles wide, while the bay itself is about ten miles across. Then in his atlas Dudley incorporates this same detail, again at latitude 38°, on his finished chart of the coast, *Carta Particulare XXXIII*; however here he expands the bay to a diameter of about twenty miles. And on the same chart, at 44°, recalling the latitude given by the *Anonymous Narrative* for Drake's careenage, he places an anchor in another bay with the inscription *il Drago Inglese*. Interestingly also, several of the placenames along his coast are

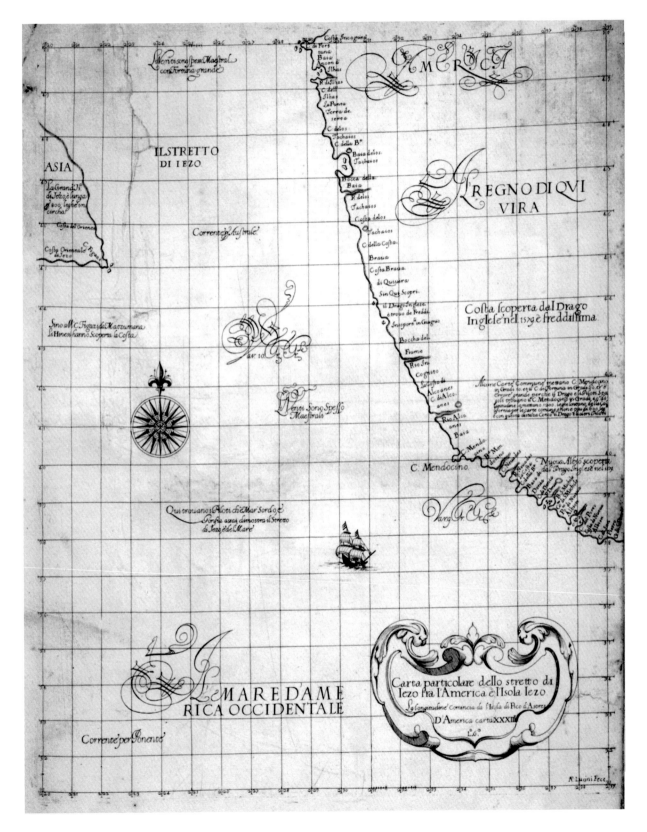

Robert Dudley's *Carta Particulare* XXXIII, 1647

toponyms which appear between latitudes 48° and 55° on Hondius' globe of 1600. It therefore appears that his charts are a composite of information from several sources, although the logic behind his amalgamation of the details remains obscure.

However, two of the features which Dudley incorporates are readily identifiable, except that again he appears not to have known precisely where and at what scale to incorporate them, as they are too large in the scale of his chart and are placed in the wrong latitudes. At the top of the chart, at latitude 50°, his coastline comes to an abrupt end above a distinctive headland that Dudley calls *C. di Fortuna*, which is the name placed at this latitude by Plancius on his 1590 map. Comparison of this feature with a modern chart, however, establishes that its shape is identical to Cape Flattery, actually situated at 48° 23', at the entrance to the Strait of Juan de Fuca.[4] Evidently Dudley knew that Drake had been at a 'stormy cape' at 50°, but mistakenly assumed that the drawing of Cape Flattery which he copied was this cape. Then above 49° he depicts a large bay that is easily recognized as Grays Harbour, which is actually located at 47°. It appears then that Dudley must have found among either his father's or Cavendish's papers copies of these details which had been taken from an illustrated journal of Drake's voyage, and although he apparently did not find any drawings of the coast beyond 48°, those which he did find are extremely valuable.

Sir William Monson was another member of the generation who went to sea in Drake's later years. He joined Elizabeth's navy around 1585 and was a captain by 1589, thereafter rising to the rank of Admiral. A few years prior to his death in 1643 he organized his papers, knowledge and opinions into a volume which was eventually published in 1704.[5] The work, 400 pages in length, is a rich mine of information on naval developments through the 16th and early 17th centuries. Several of Monson's tracts contain interesting comments on Drake, with whom he evidently was acquainted, and on his voyage. Unquestionably Monson was thoroughly familiar with Hakluyt's writings. In his own account of Drake's voyage, however, he states:

> From the 16th of April till the 5th of June, he sail'd without seeing land and arriv'd in 48 Degrees, thinking to find a passage into our Seas, which Land he named Albion; the People were courteous, and took his Men for Gods; they live in great extremity of Cold and Want; Here they trim'd their Ship, and departed the 25th of July, 1579, standing his Course for the Moluccos.[6]

Monson had to have taken these details from *The World Encompassed*, except that account does not say that Nova Albion was in 48°; and further, he does not give the latitude of Drake's careenage. Another comment in particular suggests that he knew more about the voyage than he reveals. In his introduction to the voyage he

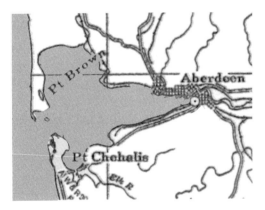

Two of the details in Dudley's map

examines Drake's career, comparing his imperfections to his perfections. Regarding Drake's perfections, Monson cites his conquest of Magellan's Strait, which he says "were counted so terrible in those days that the very thoughts of attempting it were dreadful". Then he says of Drake's northern voyage:

> But lastly, and principally, that after so many Miseries and Extremities he endur'd, and almost two years spent in unpractis'd Seas, when reason would have bid him sought home for his Rest, he left his known Course, *and ventur'd upon an unknown Sea in 48 Degrees, which Sea or Passage we know had been attempt'd by our Seas, but never discover'd.*[7]   (my italics)

It appears then that Monson had heard the story of Drake's voyage beyond 48°, although he does not reveal anything about it. However, he also included among his tracts *A Discourse Concerning the North-West Passage*, apparently written many years earlier, in which he explains the optimum organization of an expedition to discover the passage. This, he says, is best undertaken with three vessels: a ship to carry the equipment and supplies with which to launch the search, and two small barks to carry out the explorations. "The Two Barques must be strong and short, because of their aptness to stay and Tack if they come into a narrow Streight, shole Water, or amongst Ice".[8]

Monson's scheme of a ship carrying the supplies and equipment for two small vessels which would perform the explorations probably dates from the English voyages in search of the passage in the early part of the 17th century. Nevertheless it is interesting to note that in addition to the little Spanish bark which Drake brought from Central America, he very probably also had the use of a pinnace on the northwest coast of America. *The World Encompassed* says that he carried four dismantled pinnaces in the *Golden Hinde*, and probably there were more on the *Elizabeth*. When assembled, these were light, fast sailing craft of 8 to 15 tonnes displacement. He assembled one of them on the coast of Africa and, it appears, the second one before entering Magellan's Strait. Then on the coast of Chile he set up another, which he used to scout ahead until he gave it to the crew of the little bark which he seized at the island of Cano in Costa Rica. Given the overriding importance of his northern explorations it is not unreasonable to believe that he would have saved at least one of his pinnaces for this purpose and assembled it when he reached northwest America. Notably however, the English accounts do not mention a pinnace or the Spanish bark in relation to his northern voyage, and John Drake appears to have admitted that they also repaired the little bark at the careenage only after further interrogation. Is it possible then that the scheme which Monson describes for discovery of the passage originated with Drake? This question will be revisited in due course.

The captains of the small vessels, Monson says, must be skillful mariners and good cosmographers; men of great resolution not to be daunted by any disaster. In the event that the vessels should separate, they would "appoint a place of Meeting", and "upon either of their Returns, they appoint a certain place on shore where to leave their Letters wrapped in a Box of Lead, and in those Letters to make relation of their success".[9] And,

> The Masters must take an Oath to use their best efforts to advance the Voyage, and to keep secret the Journal: The Plate and Cards [charts and seacards], and all other Writings that concern their Navigation, must be taken from them at their coming home, and Seal'd up to present to his Majesty.[10]

From his reference to an Oath of secrecy and to the journal and charts being turned over to the crown, it may be inferred that Monson felt bound not to divulge whatever he knew about his nation's secret explorations. It appears then that even at this late date all such information was still sequestered in some repository within the government, most probably within the guarded precinct of the Privy Chamber. Then however, sometime between this point and 1776 this priceless assemblage of documents disappeared. In 1776 Captain James Cook sailed on his last great voyage of exploration, which was launched for the express purpose of locating the Pacific entrance to the northwest passage. According to his secret instructions, issued by the Lords of the Admiralty, Cook was to

> proceed in as direct a course as you can to the coast of Nova Albion, endeavouring to fall in with it in the latitude of 45° 0' North ... Upon your arrival on the coast of Nova Albion you are ... to proceed northward along the coast, as far as latitude 65°, or farther ... and to explore, such rivers or inlets as may appear to be of considerable extent and pointing towards Hudsons or Baffins Bays.[10]

Evidently the Admiralty did not believe that Nova Albion was located in latitude 38°. Beyond this however, it appears that they knew little more about its location than it lay somewhere north of 45°. However, thanks to Drake's private maps, to the leavings of Hondius, Molyneux and others who were involved in his commemorative project, and to his apparently unauthorized leaks via the maps of Ortelius and Plancius, much more information of his northern voyage has survived than previously supposed.

John Meares' reception at Cape Flattery by the Makah Indians, 1788

By Permission of The British Library

CHAPTER SEVEN

Tracing Drake's Explorations

Based on the foregoing analysis, it is now possible to gain a surprisingly coherent and detailed view of Drake's explorations. We begin with his course from Guatulco onto the northwest coast, and the question of his first landfall. Hakluyt gives the sailing distance as 600 leagues and later 800 leagues, but it is obvious that these figures are contrived to conceal the more northerly voyage. Indeed, beginning at Guatulco even the latter figure would barely bring Drake to latitude 43°, and then only if he had sailed up the coast against the prevailing wind. Moreover, Hakluyt describes this as a 'Spanish course', and as R.P. Bishop points out, Drake certainly would not have formed any such idea from the Spanish pilots he had interrogated.[1]

The problem the Spanish discovered when they reached the Pacific coast of America is that the prevailing winds blow down the coasts, from higher latitudes toward the equator. Therefore to attempt to reach higher latitudes by following the coast meant sailing against the wind, which for the square-rigged ships of the day involved laboriously tacking to and fro to make any headway. Initially voyages from Callao, in latitude 12° S, to Valparaiso at 33° S took many weeks. The problem was finally solved in 1563 by pilot Juan Fernandez, who found that by sailing from Callao well out to sea on the tradewinds and then working his way to the southwest until the wind swung around to a westerly he could reach Valparaiso in just twenty days.[2] Thus Fernandez had exploited the counter-clockwise circulation of winds south of the equator, and no doubt Drake learned all about this from the numerous pilots whom he captured along the coast of Chile and Peru.

Then on the coast of Central America Drake had the good fortune to capture two pilots who were carrying the official charts and sailing directions with which they were to conduct the new Viceroy to the Philippines. In the Manila trade, the Spanish made their way to between latitudes 12° and 14° N where they picked up the tradewinds and then sailed 'in longitude', that is, without altering their latitude, due westward in a straight line right across the Pacific. Then for the return voyage, as Friar Urdaneta discovered in 1565, it was necessary to work their way north from the Philippines until they picked up the westerlies between 35° and 40°N, which carried them back across the North Pacific to 'the Californias', where the wind then swung down the coast toward Mexico. Thus Urdaneta had exploited the clockwise circulation of winds north of the equator, and on examining the sailing directions carried by his captured Manila pilots Drake no doubt saw the implications for his objective of reaching a high latitude on the northwest coast of America. In order to do so expeditiously, it would be necessary to take a 'Spanish course', that is, to sail due westward on their course for the Philippines until he picked up a wind which would allow him to begin working his way northward. *The World Encompassed* states that from Guatulco, at latitude 15° N,

> we departed ... Aprill 16, setting our course directly into the sea, whereon we sayled 500 leagues in longitude, to get a winde: and betweene that and Iune 3, 1400 leagues in all, till we came into 42 deg. of North latitude

At three miles to the league then, they sailed some 1500 miles to the west before they were able to turn northward. Then from that point, subtracting this first leg, the account allows them to have sailed a further 900 leagues, or 2700 miles, to reach latitude 42°. But then it says that this was the latitude where they suddenly encountered a cold front, and that two degrees further north, at 44°, things began to freeze, and it is impossible to conceive of such conditions occurring offshore in this latitude in the month of June. Evidently then, the cold front has been arbitrarily shifted to this latitude to form part of the excuse for them turning back at 48°. In his testimony to the Inquisition at Sante Fe in 1584, John Drake related that

> they left Aquatulco ... in April and they went to seaward. They sailed continually to the northwest and north-northeast. They travelled for all of April and May, until the middle of June. From the said Aquatulco, which is in 15 degrees, they went to 48 degrees. They met with great storms along the way.

Here apparently the Spanish scribe has adjusted Drake's dates forward by ten days because the English were still working from the Julian calendar whereas Catholic Europe had switched to the new Gregorian calendar. In any case, although young Drake speaks of "great storms", he makes no mention of cold weather. Then when he was brought before the Inquisition at Lima he told them

> They sailed a thousand leagues up to the latitude of forty-four degrees, always sailing close to the wind. After this the wind changed and they went to the Californias. They discovered land in forty-eight degrees.

Bishop explains that from the point where they turned northward a course northwest and then north-northeast, 'always sailing close to the wind' for 1000 leagues would carry them very efficiently around the vortex of winds known as *Fleurieu's Whirlpool*, which is anchored more or less permanently to the west of California.[3] Then at 44°, John Drake says, the wind changed and they were obliged to alter their course. Evidently this is where they met the great storms he mentioned earlier. Most probably these came from the northwest, so now they would likely

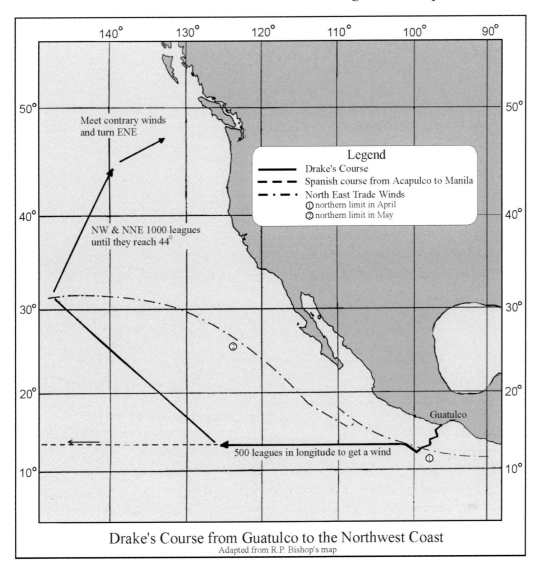

Meet contrary winds
and turn ENE

NW & NNE 1000 leagues
until they reach 44°

Legend
Drake's Course
Spanish course from Acapulco to Manila
North East Trade Winds
① northern limit in April
② northern limit in May

500 leagues in longitude to get a wind

Guatulco

Drake's Course from Guatulco to the Northwest Coast
Adapted from R.P. Bishop's map

alter their course to an east-northeast heading, which would, as Bishop concludes, bring them to a landfall in the vicinity of Vancouver Island.

The World Encompassed states that they were "forced by contrary windes to runne in with the shoare ... and to cast anchor in a bad bay ... where we were not without some danger by reason of the many gusts and flawes", and implies that this bay was in latitude 48°, which would be near Cape Flattery. And the maps of Ortelius (1587) and Plancius place a 'cape of worries' at this latitude. However, there is no bay where Drake would have considered anchoring in strong winds to be found anywhere near Cape Flattery. Probably 'cape of worries' was placed at 48° to tie the information in these maps indicating more northerly explorations back to the northernmost point which would be cited in Drake's intended account of the voyage. Deciphering the Drake Mellon map, Drake's landfall is depicted as being at latitude 50° on the outer coast of Vancouver Island. Also this is the first latitude noted and then covered over in the *Anonymous Narrative*, and both Plancius and Dudley place a 'cape of storms' at 50°. Here Cape Cook juts ten miles to seaward, and Checleset Bay on its south side offers some shelter in a northwesterly gale. But the bay is exposed to the west and south and lined with reefs, and Drake would have spent some anxious hours at anchor here. Here then is Drake's 'bad bay'.

Then when the winds died down they were becalmed by "most uile, thicke, and stinking fogges", and this is typical along the outer coast of Vancouver Island, where cold water upwelling from the depths produces thick fogs. This was the territory of the Nuu Chah Nulth people. In their oral history they still have clear memories of Captain James Cook, the Spanish and other Europeans who visited them in the latter part of the 18th century. Among the Nuu Chah Nulth clans however, the Checleset band who reside near Cape Cook have a different *potlatch* ceremony which they say relates to a visit by strange, 'hairy men' who arrived in a great 'floating house' many generations before Captain Cook. It is the tradition of the other clans to award their first gift to the most honoured guest at the potlatch. But in the case of the Checleset band, the first gift is carried to the sea and dedicated to 'the great chief' who visited from beyond the horizon long before Cook.[4] It appears then that Drake may have visited them and refilled some of his watercasks, but it is unlikely he lingered.

Then they would resume their journey, most probably sailing on a broad reach to the northwest, and the latitude in the *Anonymous Narrative* is next changed to 53°, which would place them on the outer coast of the Queen Charlotte Islands. Notably, Hondius labels the coast in this latitude 'coast of objections', recalling the passage in *The World Encompassed* about the 'frozen zone' where Drake's men 'did grievously complain' about the growing cold. The description of a sudden chill followed by freezing rain is in fact consistent with the conditions found at the edge of a freezing air mass where the opposing warm air pushes up over the leading edge of heavier cold air. As previously said it is inconceivable that these conditions could have been experienced in latitudes 42° to 44°. However, Plancius places 'frozen land' at 54°, and so here again it appears that the latitudes in the published accounts were derived by subtracting 10° from the actual. Even at 54° however, there is no case of freezing weather in June in the modern record, although there are frequent, strong outflows of freezing air off the mainland mountains to the northeast here through the winter months. The explanation: climatologists have established that the 1570's were among the coldest years at the onset of the Little Ice Age, a period of significantly cooler global climate which lasted nearly 300 years, into the middle of the 19th century.[5] It appears then that in 1579 the coast from 54° northward was immersed in

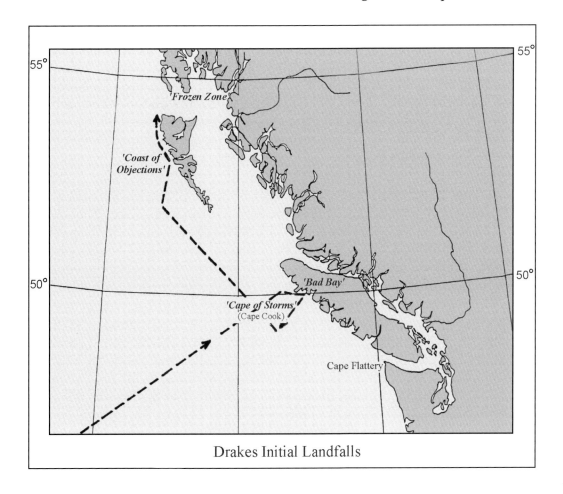

Drakes Initial Landfalls

a protracted winter, and the lengthy description of the conditions which Drake encountered may therefore be of considerable value to historical climatologists.

The World Encompassed states that they encountered the cold front offshore on 3 June and then anchored in the bad bay on 5 June, but it appears that along with shifting the cold weather 10° southward the simple expedient of reversing the dates was adopted. Most probably Drake made his initial landfall at Cape Cook on 3 June and then encountered the cold front offshore in latitude 52°, as he drew abreast of the Queen Charlotte Islands on 5 June. Then he made his second landfall at latitude 53° on the outer coast of the Queen Charlottes, where his men began to complain about the intensifying cold. At 54° a cape is noted and here Drake would reach the northwest tip of the Queen Charlottes and discover broad Dixon Entrance leading due eastward. 'Inlet of the islands' is noted, and 'strong currents' is consistent with the large tides ebbing and flooding through Dixon Entrance. Now fully exposed to the cold winds flowing out from the mountains and glaciers to the north, they would feel a deeper chill. The Haida Indians have resided at this northwest tip of the Queen Charlottes for several thousand years. In the journey around South America Drake frequently stopped to befriend and barter with the Indians, and conceivably he did so here.[6] Regardless, he would now begin to have frequent contact with the Indians of this northwest coast and he must have been impressed by the ingenuity and artistry expressed in their great seagoing canoes, massive post and beam houses and elaborately carved totem poles.

Often during outflows of cold air either the skies are clear or the overcast is at a high elevation, and if so they would now have a magnificent amphitheatre laid before them.[7] To the northeast and stretching northward the mountains of the mainland coast form a long, majestic embankment; and in the foreground they would see the lower mass of Prince of Wales Island, suggesting a passage leading north behind its southward-pointing cape. As they drew nearer they would discover that this headland is surmounted by an unforgettably distinctive feature—a great pinnacle of rock in the shape of a perfect cone rising to an elevation of 300 feet.[8] The Spanish explorers later named this headland Cape Chacon, and it stands in latitude 54° 41', marking the entrance to Clarence Strait. Plancius was given 'white cape' at 55° and Hondius places a Cape *de Fortuna* at this latitude, probably in the context of 'good fortune'. Identification of the northernmost island in the chain depicted on the Dutch Drake map as Prince of Wales Island establishes that Drake must have sailed the length of Clarence Strait. And from the fate of Cavendish's captive Spanish pilot after he was found with a letter referring to 'the North-west passage, standing in 55°', it appears that initially at least, Drake saw Cape Chacon as the beginning of the Strait of Anian.

Now as they entered Clarence Strait they would encounter a new set of conditions. The strait is essentially a long trough flanked on the west side by Prince of Wales Island, whose mountains rise to an elevation of between 2,000 and 2,500 feet, and on the east side by the much higher mountains of the mainland, around which immense glacial fields have accumulated over countless millennia. Intersecting this trough are long fjords which cut deep into the mainland, and it is through these fjords that cold air intermittently surges into the archipelago from the high glacial fields. Thus, the heavy cold air flowing out of the fjords would be trapped in Clarence Strait, as would the moisture accumulating in the air from the melting of snow on the adjacent slopes. Consequently the strait would have been overlain with cold air and fogs which would only be flushed out by more cold air pouring off the glaciers. *The World Encompassed* retains Fletcher's description of the scene:

hence come those thicke mists and most stinking fogges, which increase so much the more, by how much higher the [north] pole is raised: wherein a blind pilot is as good as the best director of a course, For the sunne striuing to performe his naturall office, in eleuating the vapors out of these inferior bodies, draweth necessarily abundance of moisture out of the sea; but the nipping cold ... meeting and opposing the Sunnes endeauor, forces him to giue ouer his worke imperfect; and instead of higher eleuation, to leaue in the lowest region, wandring vpon the face of the earth and waters as it were a second sea, through which its owne beames cannot possibly pierce, vnlesse sometimes when the sudden violence of the winds doth helpe to scatter and breake through it; which happeneth very seldome, and when it happeneth is of no continuance.

The strait continues to the northern end of Prince of Wales Island and then veers northeast a short distance before coming to the delta of the Stikine River, at latitude 56° 40'. However, Drake would now encounter an obstacle. The Stikine's vast delta of tidal marshes stretches across the strait, all but blocking it. The only navigable channel past the delta is narrow Dry Strait, so named because it drains at low tide. Dry Strait runs for some 9 miles along the outer edge of the delta before joining wide Fredrick Sound to the north. With no leeway to tack, it would be necessary to tow the ships through this narrow passage, and the *Golden Hinde* would become grounded at low water before they could move the length of the channel. Moreover, it appears there may have been another problem. Where Drake's track northward terminates on his private commemorative maps an inscription states "turned back because of the ice". Notably, when the Russians explored southeastern Alaska in the 1740's the coastal glaciers were much further advanced than in the modern era, and in the conditions described Dry Strait may well have been clogged with ice calved by le Conte Glacier, immediately to the north of the delta, and by other tidewater glaciers further north.

Drake would have no choice but to retreat from the Stikine Delta. Here then is the northernmost 'river of the straits'. However, he would not have come this far only to give up at the first obstacle, and so now he would sail westward through Sumner Strait, crossing the northern tip of Prince of Wales Island. From Sumner Strait there are openings to two narrow passages leading northward, but their entrances are obscure. Sumner Strait then turns southward between Prince of Wales and Kuiu Islands. Then at the southern extremity of Kuiu Island, latitude 56°, Drake would round Cape Decision and discover 12 mile wide Chatham Strait leading due northward, enclosed on its west side by long Baranof Island. Now however, he would be heading into the wind again and very possibly encountering ten and twenty ton blocks of ice drifting southward from Glacier Bay.

To save time manoeuvring his ships, Drake would want to assemble his remaining pinnace at the first opportunity, but the few sheltered harbours with a suitable beach would be inhabited by Indians. *The World Encompassed* describes some Indians somewhere in this 'frozen zone' who are dressed in warm furs, yet huddling together and 'sheltring under a lee banke' if possible to avoid the cold wind. In all probability this was where Drake stopped to assemble his pinnace. This was the territory of the Tlingit Indians, and their descendants say that their people traded with strange visitors for iron many generations before the arrival of the Russians.[9]   There is no clue to the location of this place in the surviving record of the voyage, but other information has led to a particular harbour.

In 1954 a man was camped in a small bay near the entrance to Chatham Strait while doing some prospecting when he found at low tide some stones which appeared to have pre-Columbian human markings of Central or South American origin—possibly discharged ballast stones. Then later that summer he found behind the beach a small, heavy metal plate with a strange inscription on it.[10]   The plate measured approximately six inches by eight inches by three quarters of an inch in thickness and was made of lead, perhaps mixed with some silver as it was nearly black. In the corners were square holes filled with rust, indicating that it had once been nailed to something. Unable to make out the inscription, he took the plate to the Smithsonian Institute while visiting Washington on business in 1956. As he watched, two members of the staff transcribed the inscription, which said something to the effect that Francis Drake herewith claimed possession of this country in the name of Queen Elizabeth. However, they told the gentleman that it had to be a fake as it was impossible for Drake to have been anywhere near Alaska. When he then got a similar reaction from the curator of the Juneau Museum, he put the plate and the handwritten transcript given to him at the Smithsonian away in a trunk, which unfortunately was stolen from a storehouse 20 years later.

The published accounts state that Drake's proclamation of Nova Albion was inscribed on a plate of 'brass', but this could simply mean an imperishable metal. The *Anonymous Narrative* on the other hand states that it was a plate of lead. And in the Conyer's manuscript, Francis Fletcher says that Drake had him inscribe a plate of lead to be left at the Pacific entrance to the Strait of Magellan. It therefore appears that they must have nailed these plates up in a number of places. Sadly, the one which the gentleman found at the entrance to Chatham Strait now appears lost, but at least we now know what one of them looked like. Moreover, the site where it was found can now be investigated by archaeologists. Also, there was a Tlingit Indian village very nearby, and it is possible that articles left by Drake may be unearthed there.

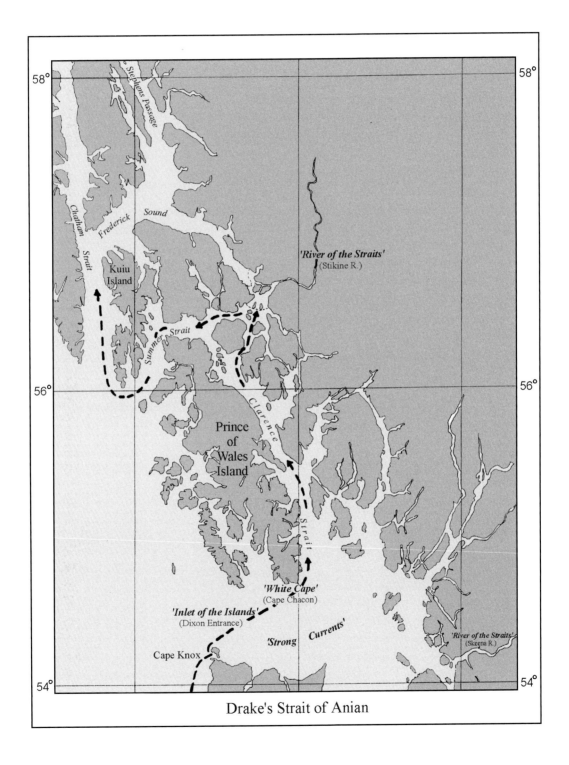

Drake's Strait of Anian

It would only have been three or four days' work to assemble the pinnace.[11] Then before turning back Drake would likely have taken it some distance up the strait, where he would discover that it forks at Admiralty Island with both branches, Chatham Strait and Stephens Passage, continuing northward to the horizon. Regardless, it is clear that he was convinced he had found the Strait of Anian, and this could only have been Chatham Strait. To this point, a number of toponyms have been identified which mark Drake's progress northward:

DRAKE NORTHBOUND
(start at bottom)

Lat.	Feature/Toponym	Source	Modern Name
57½°	River of the straits	*Ortelius 1587*	Stikine River (56° 40')
55°	Northwest Passage	*Hakluyt 1600*	Clarence Strait
	Cape of good fortune	*Hondius 1600*	Cape Chacon (54° 41')
	White Cape	*Plancius 1590*	" "
	Strong Currents	*Ortelius 1589*	" "
54°	Inlet of the Islands	*Hondius 1600*	Dixon Entrance
	Frozen Land	*Plancius 1590*	(N. side Dixon Ent.)
	Strong Currents	*Ortelius 1587*	Dixon Entrance
	Cape Mendocino	*Ortelius 1587*	Cape Knox (54° 10')
53°	Coast of Objections	*Hondius 1600*	Queen Charlotte Is.
	(second landfall)	*Anonymous Narrative*	" "
50°	Cape of storms	*Dudley 1647*	Cape Cook (50° 08')
	Cape Mendocino	*Hondius 1600*	" "
	Cape of storms	*Plancius 1590*	" "
	Cape of worries	*Ortelius 1589*	" "
	(first landfall)	*Anonymous Narrative*	" "

Now the remaining toponyms and other information become our guide to Drake's journey back down the coast. The *Anonymous Narrative* says he "turned back again, still keping along the cost as nere land as he might", but there would be no point in doubling back through Sumner and Clarence Straits and so Drake would follow the outer coast southward into Dixon Entrance. If John Drake recited the names of the 'islands of good land' in the same order that they discovered them, Drake must have given the name *Saint Bartholomew* to the Queen Charlottes and *Saint James* to Prince of Wales Island.[12] On the outer coast of *Saint James* there are numerous smaller islands including rookeries teeming with seabirds and stellar

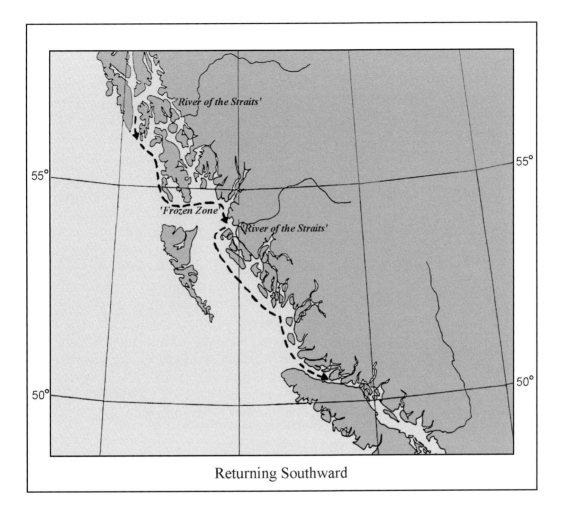

Returning Southward

sealions, and very likely they stopped here to replenish their larder. Then they would enter Dixon Entrance and pass the white cape and its distinctive spire for a second time.

Although it is misplaced by one degree at latitude 53°, the second 'river of the straits' which is noted can only be the Skeena River. *The World Encompassed* states that there was a period of fourteen days in which they were unable to observe the sun, and very possibly they were working from dead reckoning. For Drake to have found the mouth of the Skeena, he must have been curious about the eastern end of Dixon Entrance. It appears then that he was interested in the possibility of a passage eastward through the continent, as an alternative to the northern strait. Here Drake would have encountered the sizeable population of Tsimshian Indians concentrated near the river mouth because of its huge salmon resource. However, the numbers of canoes meeting them in these confined waters would have been worrisome and he would not have lingered.

At 52° is noted 'rugged coast', which indeed it is, and it may be inferred from this that Drake was interested only in the trend of the coast and did not stop to investigate its lesser openings as he continued southward. Then however, still following the mainland coast they would find themselves in a wide opening behind a great headland, funnelling into the entrance to a narrow passage—Johnstone Strait—and here again they would encounter powerful tidal flows. Here too Drake would meet the Kwakiutl people, and conceivably he learned from them by signs that the headland was a large island. Certainly he would be aware that he was now back near the latitude of their first landfall, which evidently was on the outer coast of this headland. From the mention of strong currents at 54° and 55° it is obvious that Drake regarded such instances as a primary indicator of the potential for a connection to another sea, and so very likely it was again in the hope of discovering a passage through the continent that he now began following this 'long inlet' eastward. Further support for this conclusion is provided by the detail of the strait in the Dutch Drake map, which shows a rounded embayment of the mainland coast at its eastern end that can only be Desolation Sound. It therefore appears that emerging from Johnstone Strait Drake continued probing eastward. At its eastern extremity, the narrow strait divides around some islands into several channels, all of which are notorious for their overfalls, whirlpools, and violent eddies as the tides boil through at 8 knots or more. Continuing to probe eastward, Drake probably followed Nodales and Cardero Channels into the Yucalta Rapids, and here they would have spent an anxious time waiting for the moment of slack water and then making a dash through the treacherous bottleneck.[13]

Then, following the curve of Desolation Sound they would emerge into the Strait of Georgia, and here they must have been struck by a strong sense of arrival. Suddenly this narrow, twisting labyrinth had given way to a broad inland sea, and now before them lay the long, gently sloping coastal plain of Vancouver island, its verdant forest attesting to rich soils and an abundance of life. Moreover they would notice that the air and water temperatures were now significantly warmer. What better place, Drake must have thought, than this hidden oasis for the colony which would be essential for future exploitation of the northwest passage. Ships would be able to come and go between here and the passage with little chance of detection by the Spanish, land could be cleared to grow the food needed to reprovision them, and with a limitless supply of timber the colonists could build and maintain a fleet of ships to pursue England's goals in the Pacific.

Following the coast of Vancouver Island southward some 20 miles they would find that it steps back behind a prominent point of land, Cape Lazo. From this a shoal extends to Denman Island, enclosing 15 mile long Baynes Sound. Behind the point they would see a wide bay. Its latitude is just 20' less than 50°. Taking soundings, they would find that the *Golden Hinde*, but not a larger ship, could get

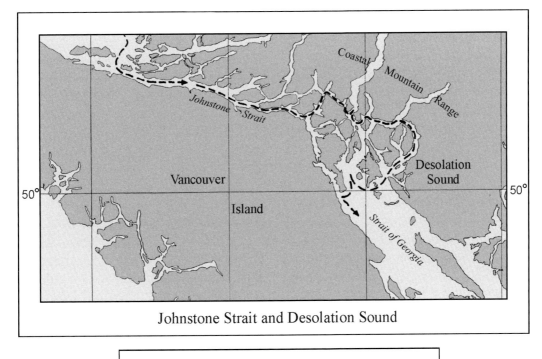

Johnstone Strait and Desolation Sound

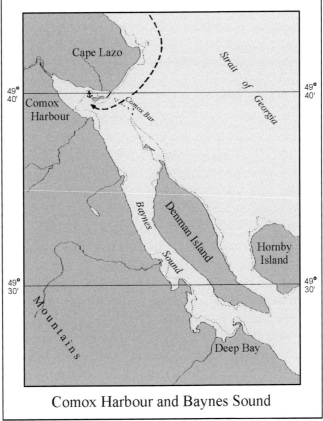

Comox Harbour and Baynes Sound

safely across the bar on high water. Here then is the basis for the term 'bay of small ships'. In Baynes Sound the Salish Indian population occupying several villages probably totalled between 1500 and 2000 persons.[14] The notation 'beautiful young women' in Drake's southern nomenclature suggests a friendly reception. The Salish name for this place was *Comox*, which meant 'plenty', and so Drake would have thought. Extending partway across the mouth of the bay is a long spit of sand which protects it from the southeast fetch. At the head of the bay there was a broad tidal marsh which could be diked to create very fertile land for planting, and beyond lay a lush valley filled with towering cedar and firs.

Drake could not have hoped for a more commodious place in which to establish a colony. Nor would he subsequently find one which offered better natural defenses against an intervention by the Spanish, should they ever discover this inland sea. A fort could be constructed on the spit guarding the harbour, and large ships would be obliged to come through the narrow entrance at the southern end of the Sound, which could be protected by a second fort. In many respects the physical arrangement of Baynes Sound and Comox Harbour at its head must have reminded Drake of Plymouth Sound, and probably he made numerous drawings to illustrate its attributes in his journal.

Here then was the first 'bay of small ships', the real bay of Nova Albion. It is clear from all of the evidence, however, that the bay where he stopped to repair the *Golden Hinde* was not on Vancouver Island, and it is not hard to understand why. Within a day or two word of the strange visitors would have brought large native contingents from other villages by canoe, and Drake would have become increasingly concerned about the security of his little company. The shores of the Georgia Basin were inhabited by a large population of Salish Indians—probably in excess of 20,000 at this time—and this scene would be repeated wherever he went in this inland sea. Drake would have considered it too risky to unload the *Golden Hinde* and beach her for repairs anywhere in the vicinity. But he must have performed an act of possession at Comox. All of the accounts, of course, place this event at the careenage, and very possibly he did so there as well. Clearly however, he would have done so at the future colony site. But what was the point of erecting a 'great post' as opposed to some other form of monument such as a rock cairn? Could it be that Drake was emulating the totem poles to which the northern tribes of this coast so obviously attached great importance?[15]

It is unlikely that Drake stayed at Comox more than three or four days at most. Then, continuing down the coast of Vancouver Island probably as far as the harbour of Nanaimo, he would have found nothing to change his opinion that Comox afforded the best shelter and natural defenses for the future colony. The next features in his southern nomenclature are a 'Point of Sardines' and a 'Point of St.

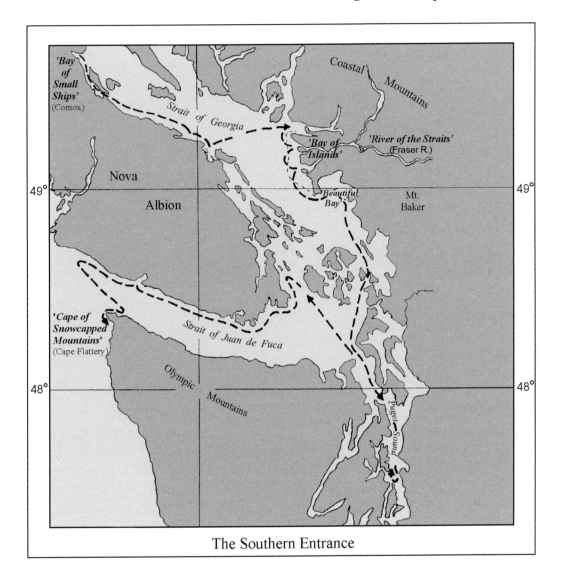

The Southern Entrance

Michael', followed by a large, double-channelled river. As previously noted, there is only one such river of any consequence on this coast, which is the Fraser, also noted as a 'river of the straits' at 49°. The coast mountains turn eastward along the north side of the Fraser, and seeing this apparent gap in the coast Drake would again be drawn by the possibility of a passage through the continent. Probably the two points of land noted are Point Atkinson and Port Grey, flanking the entrance to Burrard Inlet. The term 'bay of islands' suggests that he saw the lowlands south of the inlet as islands, as the later Spanish explorers also thought initially. Evidently however, Drake soon recognized that this was a river and not a seapassage leading eastward, and it appears that he used the pinnace to make a quick reconnaissance of the estuary.

South of the river is noted 'beautiful bay', and probably this was Boundary Bay with the towering volcano Mount Baker to the east and the San Juan Islands to the southwest. Then, sailing past the islands Drake would see the long bank of snowcapped mountains on the Olympic Peninsula, lining the Strait of Juan de Fuca westward into the Pacific. For the future defense of the colony it would be important to know whether these mountains were part of another large island in this long chain, which would mean another opening to the Pacific further south, and as will later be seen, there is evidence which suggests that he sailed some distance into Puget Sound before returning into the Strait of Juan de Fuca. Then, again with future defensive arrangements in mind, he would have followed the southern coast of Nova Albion out into the Pacific, noting the positions of its several harbours.

Before he even saw it, Cape Flattery would now have become a pivotal feature in Drake's reconnaissance. Unless he subsequently found an opening further south, this 'cape of snowcapped mountains' would mark the southernmost entrance leading to the future colony and his Strait of Anian. Eventually his men would be bound to a solemn oath of secrecy covering everything they had seen north of this cape. For the present however, he would be focused on the cape itself and its inhabitants. The cape would be the signal landmark guiding English ships into the straits, but if they failed to recognize it and turn sharply eastward, they would be in imminent peril on the treacherous outer coast of Nova Albion, so it would be essential to make careful drawings of this crucial feature. And allowing that future expeditions might encounter the inhabitants of the Cape, it would be desirable to gain their friendship. These were the Makah Indians, and from the accuracy of Dudley's detail of the cape there can be no doubt that Drake met them. Notably, part of another Makah village 14 miles south of Cape Flattery was buried in a mudslide early in the following century, and here archaeologists have unearthed from the buried houses numerous tool hafts containing pieces or traces of high carbon steel.[16]

Dudley's detail of Grays Harbour shows that Drake continued to follow the coast close inshore, and confirms that he was trying to determine if the Olympic Peninsula was another large island. To have drawn it so accurately, it appears that he must have taken the pinnace most of the way into the head of the harbour—a distance of some 15 miles. Then in Drake's southern nomenclature, the next river after the Fraser is a 'great river' flanked by 'beach' to the north and 'rugged land' to the south, and this can only be the Columbia River. Several later explorers mistook the mouth of the Columbia as a bay, and to have concluded that it was a river Drake may have sailed across the treacherous bar at its mouth, again seeking a more southerly connection to his straits.

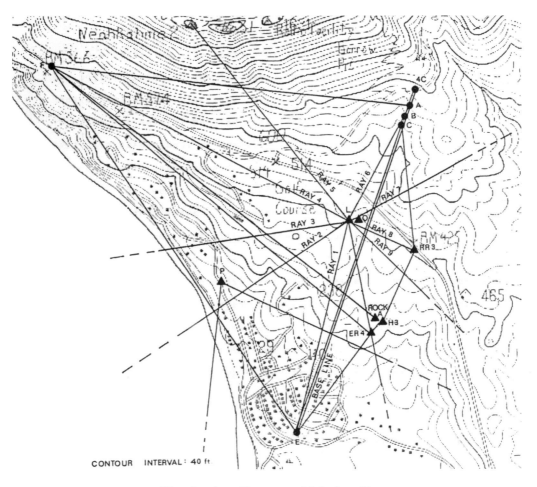

The Ancient Survey at Nehalem Bay

After 'rugged land', a 'point of position' is identified, which is an unusual choice of names considering that Drake undoubtedly took numerous sightings to establish his position in latitude as he progressed down the coast. However, when settlers began arriving in Oregon in the 19th century, the Indians told of strange visitors to Nehalem Bay, 30 miles south of the Columbia, generations earlier. Compass bearings and symbols were discovered inscribed on rocks and soon a treasure hunt began, but none was found, although a storm exposed an Elizabethan coin on the beach. Finally in the 1970's, realizing that the rocks were cairns marking an ancient survey, local historian Wayne Jenson called in the American Society of Civil Engineers to reconstruct the survey.[17] The cairns are immediately adjacent to the bay on Neahkahnie Mountain, which was regularly burned off by the Indians to create new forage for game. The survey forms a triangle approximately a mile long on each side. In addition, there are several cairns inside the triangle. Its base is a meridian derived from magnetic north, which of course has migrated somewhat since. The triangle was diagrammed on a rock with the length of its base noted in English yards. At the vertex opposite the meridian, the Latin words *deos* for 'gods' or 'heavens' and *augur* for 'predict' are inscribed a rock face.

Searching through historical records, the engineers found a solitary example which was a close comparison, drawn to scale in manuscript. This survey too is a triangle with a meridianal base, which is approximately 4,840 feet in length compared to 4,873 feet for the length of the base on Neahkahnie Mountain. It is the plan of a survey set up in England by Drake's contemporary William Bourne, whose method for determining longitude was described in the diary of Richard Madox.[18] The engineers assumed that the Neahkahnie survey was for the purpose of establishing a boundary, but 'point of position' surely is a reference to position in longitude. Evidently Bourne had set up the prime meridian in England and Drake was attempting to determine the longitude of this coast, in order to gauge the sailing distance through the northwest passage. Very possibly Fenton was to stop here and replicate Drake's observations, to check his calculations.[19]

After 'point of position', now identified as Nehalem Bay at latitude 45° 46', the next place in Drake's southern nomenclature is the second 'bay of small ships', also labelled 'bay of fires'. Undoubtedly this is one and the same bay which is depicted in the corner of Hondius' Broadside map, with the Indians lighting fires upon Drake's departure as described in *The World Encompassed*. Clearly this is Drake's careenage, subsequently relabelled *Portus Nova Albionis*. The *Anonymous Narrative* places Drake's careenage in latitude 44°, and in fact there is only one bay on the coast of Oregon or California which closely matches the drawing, and that is Whale Cove, situated 60 miles down the coast from Nehalem Bay at latitude 44° 45'.

Credit for finding this socalled 'lost harbour', as previously noted, belongs entirely to Bob Ward. The key, he discovered, was the significance of the little island drawn adjacent to the spit of land on the west side of the bay. The island is not a separate feature, but rather the spit itself depicted at high tide when it becomes disconnected from the mainland and takes this somewhat reduced form. Evidently it was added to the original rutter drawing as an aid from which to gauge high water in the bay.[20] Realizing the meaning of the diagram, Ward searched the coast for a bay with a tidal spit like this and found Whale Cove. Then he found that some two dozen topographical features in the drawing matched those at the cove. For example, near the ship there is an Indian who appears to have lit a fire in the water, but at Whale Cove there is a dry rock near the shore in this location. The Indians' dwellings are described as conical log and earth-covered pit houses. The type, known as a *kickwilli*, was commonplace in the interior of British Columbia through Oregon, but on the coast has been found only between the Columbia River and Cape

Drake's Careenage

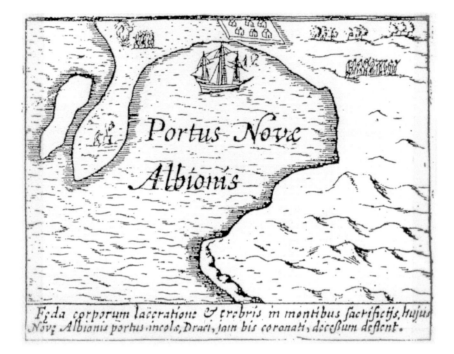

The drawing on Hondius' Broadside map
By Permission of The British Library

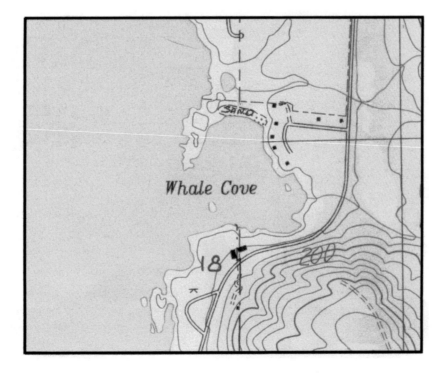

Whale Cove, latitude 44° 45' on the coast of Oregon
Adapted from the USGS Survey

Courtesy of Keith Garnett

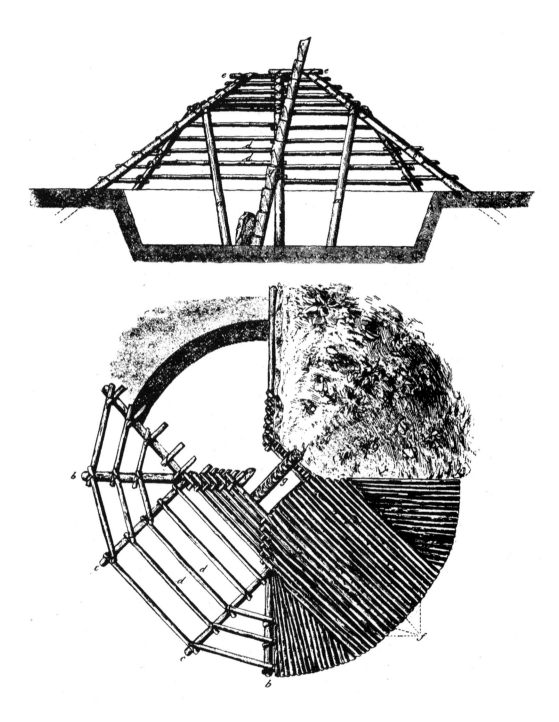

A *kickwilli* pithouse

Mendocino.[21] Ward also explains that the description in the accounts of a strange animal which Drake's men called a 'conie' matches precisely the characteristics of the *muskrat*, which were plentiful in this area but whose habitat did not extend south of Cape Mendocino.

The World Encompassed describes the Indians at the careenage in considerable detail. At first they gathered at a distance to watch Drake's men, but soon they accepted his invitation to lay down their arms and then the camp was visited by a large assemblage who presented him with a 'crown'—no doubt a ceremonial headdress. Then, when the *Golden Hinde* was repaired and reloaded, Drake and some of his men trekked inland with their hosts, visiting several villages and hunting: "infinite was the company of very large and fat Deere which there we sawe by thousands, as we supposed, in a heard". Undoubtedly these 'fat deer' were Roosevelt Elk, and to have seen such numbers it appears they may have travelled some 20 miles through the coastal mountains into the Willamette Valley. Then, the account says, with everything in readiness and the Indians apparently saddened and "making fires before and behind and on each side", they set sail.

The World Encompassed states that Drake arrived at his careenage on June 17 and departed on July 23. Obviously it would have been impossible to perform the aforementioned explorations between June 3, which appears to be a reliable date for his initial landfall at Cape Cook, and June 17. The *Anonymous Narrative*, however, states that Drake departed the careenage at "the latter end of August". In all probability then, the dates in *The World Encompassed* have been altered by the simple expedient of changing the month. Most probably the true dates for Drake's arrival and departure are July 17 and August 23 respectively, leaving him 44 days for these explorations prior to his arrival here. But is this reasonable? According to the foregoing reconstruction of his explorations, between Cape Cook and Whale Cove Drake would have travelled approximately 2,000 nautical miles. Deducting, say, ten days for the intermediate stops described means that through the remaining thirty-four days he had to have sailed, on average, about 60 miles per day. This is a reasonable allowance considering that much of his journey northward from Cape Cook was probably 24 hour sailing, and that the largest part of the journey was southbound with the wind at his back. Nevertheless the reconnaissance which Drake performed in that time was a remarkable feat and is great testimony to both his seamanship and his capacity for decision-making.

DRAKE'S JOURNEY SOUTHWARD
(start at top)

Lat.		Feature/Toponym	Source	Modern Name
53°		river of the straits	*Ortelius 1589*	Skeena River (54° 09')
52°		rugged coast	*Hondius 1600*	(mainland)
51°		long inlet	*Hondius 1600*	Johnstone Strait
50°	*	bay of small ships,	*Ortelius* 1589	Comox Harbour (49° 40')
		also beautiful women	*Ortelius 1589*	" "
		beautiful bay	*Plancius 1590*	" "
		Nova Albion	*Molyneux 1603*	Vancouver Island
49°		river of the straits	*Ortelius 1587*	Fraser River (49° 16')
	*	point of small fish	*Ortelius 1589*	Point Atkinson (49° 20')
	*	point St. Michael	*Ortelius 1589*	Point Grey (49° 16')
	*	bay of islands	*Ortelius 1589*	Fraser R. Delta
	*	double channel river (detail)	*Ortelius 1589*	Fraser River (49° 06')
	*	beautiful bay	*Ortelius 1589*	Boundary Bay
		mountainous land	*Hondius 1600*	(mainland)
48°		cape of worries	*Ortelius 1587*	Cape Flattery (48° 23')
		cape Mendocino	*Ortelius 1589*	" "
		cape of worries	*Plancius 1590*	" "
		cape of snowcapped mountains	*Hondius 1600*	" "
		cape (detail)	*Molyneux 1603*	" "
		cape (detail)	*Dudley 1647*	" "
47°		bay (detail)	*Dudley 1647*	Grays Harbour (46° 54')
46°	*	beach	*Ortelius 1589*	(N. of Columbia R.)
	*	great River	*Ortelius 1587 & 1589*	Columbia River (46° 15')
		rugged coast	*Ortelius 1589*	(S. of Columbia R.)
	*	rugged land	*Ortelius 1589*	" "
	*	point of position	*Ortelius 1589*	Nehalem Bay (45° 46')
44°		beautiful bay	*Ortelius 1589*	Whale Cove (44° 45')
	*	bay of small ships,		" "
		also bay of fires	*Ortelius 1589*	" "

* see also Chapter IV, p.61

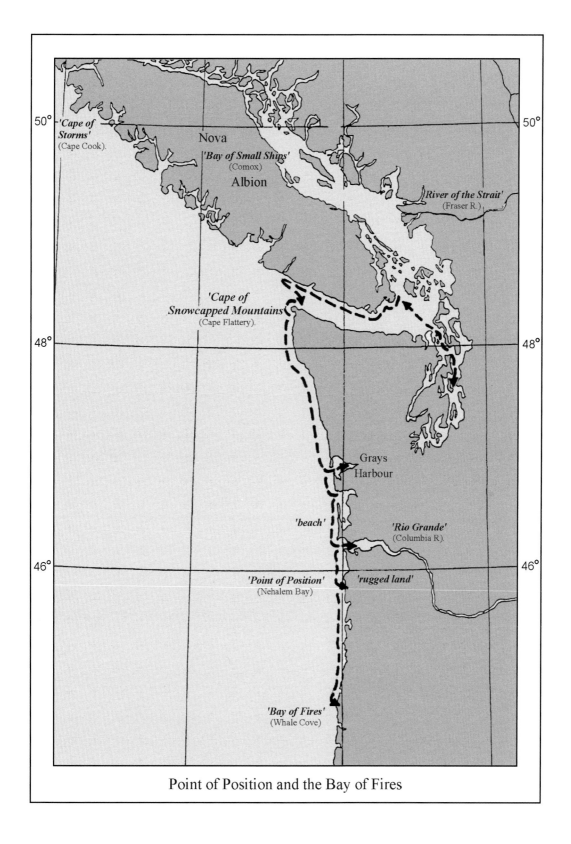

Point of Position and the Bay of Fires

Measuring the angular distance between moon and star

CHAPTER EIGHT

An Old Sailor's Yarn

Not long after news of Drake's death reached England in April 1596, the government received a curious new proposal for discovery of the northwest passage. Martin Frobisher's former associate Michael Lok was residing in Venice at the time, and that month he chanced to meet an "ancient Pilot of Ships", a Greek named Juan de Fuca, who rekindled his interest in the subject with a remarkable story of his own discovery of the passage.[1] De Fuca, whose real name was Apostolos Valerianos, was returning to his homeland after 40 years' service with the Spanish in the New World. He told Lok that he was on the Manila Galleon which Cavendish had captured at Cabo San Lucas in 1587, and had lost goods of his own worth sixty thousand ducats. Then, he said, he was the pilot of three ships which the Viceroy of Mexico sent out to discover the Strait of Anian and fortify it to prevent its use by the English; but the voyage was cut short on account of a threatened mutiny. However, he said he was sent out again and this time he discovered

> a broad inlet of Sea, betweene 47 and 48 degrees of Latitude ... and very much broader Sea then was at the said entrance .. [and] he being entred thus farre into the said Strait, and being come into the North Sea already ... hee therefore set sayle and returned homewards againe towards Nova Spania, where he arrived at Acapulco, Anno 1592.[2]

De Fuca said when he returned the Viceroy promised a reward for his service, but after two years none was forthcoming and so he went to Spain, where he was received at the King's court, but again the promise was unfulfilled. The reason, he concluded, was that the Spanish understood the English had now given up their voyages for the discovery of the northwest passage, and therefore his services were no longer needed. However, if the Queen of England would restore the value of the goods which Cavendish had seized from him and furnish him with "one ship of fortie tunnes burden and a Pinnasse", he could complete the discovery of the Northwest Passage "in thirtie dayes time, from one end to the other of the Streights".[3]

Lok wrote to Lord Burghley and to Sir Walter Raleigh and Richard Hakluyt recounting de Fuca's story and seeking funds to bring him to England. While he did so de Fuca continued his journey home to the island of Cefalonia. But then after exchanging letters with him Lok learned that he had died. Although the Strait of Juan de Fuca was named after him by the 18th century explorers, historians have tended to discount de Fuca's story as purely apocryphal. There is no record of this voyage he describes, or of him being received at the royal court of Spain, and so his story appears to be nothing more than an attempt to defraud the English government. Nevertheless, it also appears that he was privy to Spanish intelligence of English efforts to discover the passage. Moreover, comparing his story with the picture we have now formed of Drake's explorations, there is remarkable similarity between them. The following are excerpts from de Fuca's story as retold by Lok, compared with elements of Drake's exploit [in brackets]:

> ... he followed his course in that voyage West and North-west ... all alongst the coast of Nova Spain, and California, and the Indies, now called North America ... and found that Land still trending sometime North-west [Cape Cook to the NW tip of the Queen Charlottes] and North-east [to Cape Chacon], and north [in Clarence Strait], and also East [through Johnstone Strait] and South-eastward [in the Strait of Georgia], and very much broader sea then was at said entrance, and that hee passed by divers Ilands in that sayling.

> Also he said, that he went on land in divers places, and that he saw some people on Land, clad in Beasts skins ...

> And also ... that hee not being armed to resist the force of the salvage people that might happen [Nova Albion], hee therefore set sayle ...

But here is the clincher:

> And at the entrance of this said Strait [of Anian] there is on the north-west coast thereof, a great Hedland or Island [Prince of Wales Island], with an exceeding high Pinacle, or spired Rock, like a piller thereupon [Cape Chacon, at the entrance to Clarence Strait] [4]

Clearly de Fuca's story was based on Drake's secret explorations, and there can be little doubt that this was realized and caused some consternation in England. Indeed, Admiral Monson mentions in his memoirs that he heard all about it.[5] How then did de Fuca come to possess this knowledge? Notably, Drake captured a Greek pilot they called Juan Greco at Valparaiso, but then he set him free outside Callao, long before he sailed into the North Pacific. Then Francis Pretty says that Cavendish too captured a Greek pilot on the coast of Chile although his account, which appears to misname the Greek "George", does not say where they let him go.[6] In all probability these Greeks were one and the same Juan de Fuca. His claim of having lost 60,000 ducats probably relates to the gold which Drake took from his ship at Valparaiso rather than the Manila galleon captured by Cavendish. And most probably da Fuca's claim to have been on the galleon was a fabrication, although

Cavendish very likely did put him ashore at Cabo San Lucas with his captives from the galleon. If so, then de Fuca must have made the acquaintance of Juan Sebastion Vizcaino, a Spanish adventurer whom Cavendish set ashore from the galleon.[7] And if, as appears likely, de Fuca went on the first voyage he described, when the mutiny occurred, then they must have met again because Vizcaino commanded that expedition, which actually sailed in 1594.[8]

In 1602 the Viceroy sent Vizcaino out again, and on this voyage he was accompanied by a Friar, Antonio de la Ascension, who later wrote that the secret object of the expedition was to discover the Strait of Anian.[9] And behind this quest lay another remarkable story which Ascension told to a colleague, who published a memoir about it. Ascension told him that a foreign pilot named Morera had accompanied Drake on his voyage.[10] This is independently corroborated by a Spanish official who was present at Guatulco and wrote a letter naming Morera before Drake sailed for northwest America.[11] According to Ascension's colleague:

> When the Captain Francisco Draque returned to his country, this pilot—who had come emerging from the Strait [of Anian] in his company—was very sick ... and to see if the airs of the land would give him life, as a dead thing they put him ashore. The which [pilot] in a few days recovered health and walked through the land for the space of four years. He came forth to N.M. [New Mexico] and from there to Santa Barbara [in Chihuahua], and then passed to the mines of Sombrerete
>
> ... he had travelled ... more than 500 leagues of mainland, until he came far enough to catch sight of an arm of the sea. ... The pilot told how this arm of the sea runs from north to south; and that it seemed to him that it went on to the northward to connect with the harbour where the Englishman had put him ashore. And that on the sea coast he had seen many good harbours and great inlets; and that from the point where they put him ashore he would venture to get to Spain in 40 days in a good ships-tender, and that he must go to get acquainted with the Court of England.[12]

Evidently Morera also drew a map, because Ascension subsequently produced one which obviously is related to the story. The map, published in 1622, is the first to depict California as an island, which it then became on many maps for a century or more thereafter.[13] From the top of the Gulf of California, Ascension depicts a long seapassage reaching northward and emerging into a broader opening behind a great square headland, strongly suggesting Puget Sound and the Olympic Peninsula except that they are placed a little too far south. Here then is the arm of the sea described by Morera as running north to the harbour where he said Drake put him ashore. Further north this is followed at latitude 49° by a river—obviously the

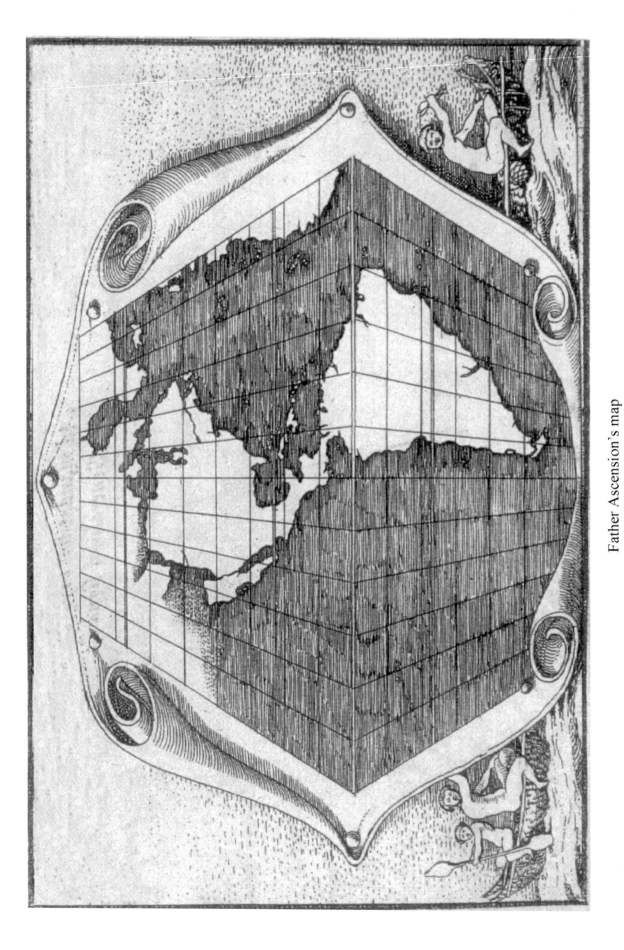

Father Ascension's map

Fraser—and then near 55° by a southward-pointing headland which would be Prince of Wales Island. And there, running northward from the headland to a junction with the northwest passage, is Drake's Strait of Anian, albeit somewhat simplified. It is impossible to know whether Morera, the Spanish authorities or Ascension omitted Vancouver Island and the Queen Charlottes. Clearly however, Morera was with Drake and the Spanish had heard all about the voyage—at least what Morera was willing to tell them—sometime around 1584. Very probably this is how the unfortunate pilot Ersola learned about "the North-west passage, standing in 55 degrees", and was consequently hanged by Cavendish.

Evidently both de Fuca and Ascension read Morera's account and saw his map, although at different times, when they were with Vizcaino.[14] It is difficult to believe, however, that Drake would simply have abandoned a member of his company on the remote northwest coast of America. Nor, as remarkable as Morera's adventure must have been, is it likely that an experienced pilot, able to navigate by the stars, would have spent four years wandering about before reaching Mexico. Moreover, it appears that he was not alone; that a significant portion of Drake's company did not cross the Pacific with him. When Philip's diligent colonial officials took depositions from Drake's released captives they made a point of asking them how many men Drake had with him, and most reported 80 or more.[15] Then when John Drake was interrogated, he admitted that only 60 men left the Pacific in the *Golden Hinde*.[16] *The World Encompassed* states that 59 reached England, one having died en route home.

It appears then that about a quarter of Drake's company are unaccounted for. And what is most interesting about the stories of de Fuca and Ascension is the common thread that one or more small ships could get through the northwest passage in a short time, and that there would be some sort of reward from the Queen of England for doing so, recalling the statement in *The World Encompassed* that Drake offered 'profitable persuasions' to bolster his men's enthusiasm for finding the short way home. Apparently Ascension's version lost some details in the retelling by his colleague, who says "a good ships-tender" could get to Spain in 40 days. De Fuca on the other hand says "one ship of fortie tunnes burden and a Pinnasse" could get through the passage in 30 days, and in fact a small bark and a pinnace are undoubtedly what Drake had at his disposal. And 20 or so of his men is what would have been required to sail them.

It very much appears then that Drake must have sent these men, including Morera, homeward through his supposed Strait of Anian. Indeed it makes perfect sense that he would attempt to complete the discovery of the passage after sailing all this way. But obviously he had decided not to do so in the *Golden Hinde*, and there can be no doubt this was a decision which his backers would have heartily supported. For Drake to have attempted the unexplored passage in the *Golden Hinde* would have put their 26 tonnes of Spanish treasure at risk. However, at the same time he was expected to use his best efforts to discover the passage, and so now he had to improvise. And certainly sending only a quarter of his men was more sensible than risking the entire company. However, the decision must have weighed heavily on him, especially after seeing the ice in the strait. No doubt this is why he probed for a passage through the continent as an alternative. In the final analysis however, he was left with no alternative, and apart from the problem of the ice, certainly the northern strait appeared to lead to the arctic sea.

But what about de Fuca's notion that one could get through the Passage in a month, could they really have thought this? Actually, yes they could have. At this point no one had any idea of the complexity of America's arctic coastline. From Ascension's map it appears that they expected the passage to run more or less in a straight line from its junction with the Strait of Anian about 3,000 miles to Frobisher's eastern entrance.[17] Moreover, it was generally believed at this time that above latitude 60° the wind blew continually from the west, and so it would not have been unreasonable for Drake to project that his men would average at least 4 knots, or 100 miles of headway daily. However, in order to sail through the passage before the icy grip of winter took hold they would have to get underway before the end of summer. And before they could do so, Drake had to find a harbour where he could safely beach the vessels for repairs and then fit out the little ones for their journey.

There certainly would not be time in the little party's dash for home to forage for their sustenance, so the trek inland from the careenage to obtain a supply of venison likely was for their benefit. Meanwhile, Drake had probably put his young cousin John to work making copies of their charts and illustrated journal for presentation to Elizabeth in case the *Golden Hinde* did not reach England. Then there would be the problem of selecting the men. Other than Morera there is no record of their names, but it would not be surprising if there was a member of the Drake-Hawkins clan among them to carry the family banner triumphantly through the passage. And finally, there would be some part of the treasure, at least of the silver, to be loaded as their crew share. But would Drake then have sent the little ships back up the coast unescorted? The case for him sending them home via his strait does not depend upon this possibility, but it merits consideration.

Interestingly, in the discussion of the 'frozen zone' *The World Encompassed* states that they "had for a long season familiar intercourse" with the Indians who dressed in furs, and that the North and North-west winds are here constant in June and July, as the North wind alone is in August and September, we ... found it by our owne experience

And elsewhere:

... hence comes it, that in the very middest of their Summer, the snow hardly departeth euen from their very doores, but is neuer taken away from their hils at all

However, the account then says that they departed from the careenage on 23 July, stopped at the "Ilands of Saint James" to harvest 'seals' and seabirds, and then set sail again on 25 July, making their first landfall in the western Pacific on 30 September. The crossing time of 68 days is specifically noted, and certainly this appears credible allowing that Cavendish, by comparison, reached the 'Ladrones' (Mariana Islands) from Cape St. Lucas in 42 days. As previously noted however, the *Anonymous Narrative* states that Drake left the careenage in "the latter ende of August" and it appears that to cover up his northern explorations the date of his departure from the careenage was subsequently altered in the published account from 23 August to 23 July. But then the narrative also goes on to state that they made their first landfall across the Pacific in "the latter ende of November", and so allowing 68 days for the Pacific crossing, he could not have left the American coast before late September.[18] It therefore appears that *The World Encompassed* actually omits two months spent on the northwest coast—one before the careenage and one afterward. So how *did* he spend this month between leaving the careenage and finally setting sail across the Pacific?

The references in *The World Encompassed* to the north wind in September and to the snow *never* leaving the hills in the frozen zone suggest that Drake escorted the little ships back to his strait. Indeed, after their experiences among the northern Indians with their swift canoes, there really would be no question of the need for him to do so. Provided they did not encounter any major storms, departing Whale Cove on 23 August and heading northwest on a broad reach he could have been at the mouth of Chatham Strait by the second week of September. There may even have been time for him to explore some distance up the outer coast beyond the entrance to Chatham Strait, which would explain the curvature of the coastline beyond 56° on Hakluyt's remarkable 1587 map. However, the other openings to his strait could easily be missed, and most probably they would return to its southern entrance. Then after launching the little ships into the strait he would turn his mind to provisions for the Pacific crossing, and so he would stop as he previously had at the lesser islands of *St. James* to stock their larder. Then, moving a little offshore and with the wind at his back, he would have made a fast return down the coast.

Drake's point of departure from the coast

As depicted on Molyneux's suppressed globe

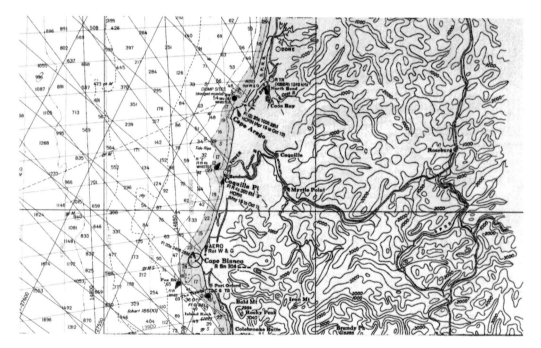

The actual coastline at latitude 43°

The other scenario, of course, is that Drake parted company with the little ships outside Whale Cove and spent the month coasting the Californias southward. On Molyneux's suppressed globe however, his track returns southward only to a *C. Mendocino* at latitude 43°, just 100 miles south of Whale Cove, before heading off across the Pacific, and here the details of the coastline are quite realistic. The cape at this latitude is Cape Arago, and immediately to the north is Coos Bay. Just to the north of his cape Molyneux depicts a bay. Then a little below 42° he notes *C. Nevado*, which could only be Cape Blanco; and between the two capes he depicts a river which also serves as a boundary, which could only be the Coquille River. Thus it appears Drake's last stop on the coast, probably for water and firewood, was at Coos Bay.[19] The *Anonymous Narrative* says they left the coast on a south-southwest heading, and from Cape Arago, an allowance of 68 days to reach their first landfall in the western Pacific is perfectly reasonable.

In all probability then, Drake did not visit the coast of present day California at all. But why not? Notably his pursuer from Peru, the great navigator Pedro Sarmiento later said that Cape Mendocino was at latitude 43°, and very probably the Spanish charts Drake seized from the Manila pilots already showed the coast up to that point.[20] Therefore all he had to do to complete his reconnaissance was to tie his own chart back to this cape on the Spanish charts. Then, combining his charts of the extremities of America with those he had seized from the Spanish for the intervening coastline, he would have the basis for a comprehensive chart of the entire Pacific coast of America. Indeed, it seems most likely that the "gran carta" which ambassador Mendoza reported Drake had given to Elizabeth upon his return was not a map of the world, but just such a chart of the Pacific coast of America, as exemplified by Hakluyt's remarkable *Novus Orbis* map of 1587.

But what became of the party Drake launched for home via his strait? Unfortunately the straits come to a dead end 180 miles to the north in Lynn Canal (at Skagway). Very possibly they were attacked by the fierce Tlingit and did not even get that far. From Morera's story however, it appears they survived and retreated down the coast. But it would be too late to catch Drake, and their ships were too small to follow him across the Pacific. And it would have been suicidal to return down the coast into Spanish waters. So they would be stranded. The only thing they could have done is to return to the relatively hospitable situation at Whale Cove and await rescue.[21] In his discourse on the northwest passage, Admiral Monson suggests that such a contingency plan would have been made, and it is hard to believe that Drake's men would have agreed to attempt the voyage without a commitment to rescue them if they didn't get through. This would explain why Drake was so anxious to get a new expedition underway immediately after he returned, and why the true location of the careenage, like that of Nova Albion, was always covered up thereafter.

In all events it appears that after two or three years of waiting at Whale Cove the stranded mariners began to despair, and so Morera, who probably was a Portuguese renegade, must have agreed to try to reach England via Mexico with an appeal for their rescue.[22] Indeed it appears that Morera invented his story of the long arm of sea running north behind California to distract the Spanish from searching the outer coast. But they would not have been favourably disposed to his hope of reaching the court of England, and not surprisingly that is the last that is heard of him. Two centuries later however, Father Crespi, the first Spaniard to explore the eastern shores of San Francisco Bay, noted on his map of the area that the Indians were "barbados, rubios y blancos" ('blond, fair complexioned and bearded')[23], and so it appears that the other stranded sailors may have trekked south and spent the remainder of their days in that area.[24] But if so, perhaps as Admiral Monson's memoirs suggest, they left a "box of lead" containing letters at Whale Cove.

Drake's Aims and Achievements

The name Sir Francis Drake is emblazoned in history as one of England's greatest heroes. His innovative and often brilliant exploits in the New World and in the defence of his homeland arguably mark the beginning of England's rise as a great seapower. And his voyage around the world has long been celebrated as one of the most remarkable maritime adventures ever. But the voyage is generally characterized as the consummate display of Drake's genius and audacity as a privateer. Almost never is he referred to as an explorer. However, the principal conclusions of this study are that the evidence examined reveals a truly extraordinary feat of exploration, and that the addition of this hitherto unrecognized achievement and its aftermath to what was previously known completely alters understanding of the voyage and obliges a reappraisal of Drake's goals and accomplishments, and indeed of the whole picture of English imperial ambitions and naval strategy toward the Pacific during Elizabeth's reign.

It is now obvious that approval for Drake's voyage was tied to an effort to fulfil the longstanding vision of a northwest passage opening the way to a great naval and commercial enterprise in the Pacific. That this mission was not merely an add-on to the goal of raiding Philip's colonies is underscored by the time taken to plan the voyage, by the special construction and equipping of Drake's ship, and by the diligence with which he performed and recorded his great reconnaissance. Clearly Drake's careful illustration of the coasts in his rutter, his interrogation of captured pilots and seizure of their charts and sailing directions, and consolidation of the information into the grand chart which he presented to Elizabeth were all part of a systematic effort to build a foundation of geographical and navigational knowledge for the larger enterprise to come. Especially interesting is the survey at the 'point of position' matching that set up in England by William Bourne. Bourne's reference to the lunar distance method of determining longitude in his manual on navigation and his development of a table of ephemerides of the moon suggest that the meridian which he established in Kent was the precursor to the prime meridian at Greenwich.

Sadly, it appears that Drake's illustrated journal and charts are lost forever. However, regarding the extent of his northern explorations the evidence in the surviving sources is compelling. Deciphering of the cryptograms in Drake's commemorative maps together with the corroborating information leaked by him to Ortelius and Plancius, and found in the globes of Molyneux and Hondius, establishes beyond any reasonable doubt that Drake discovered the major islands of the northwest coast and sailed the length of the straits separating them from the mainland as far north as the Stikine River in southeastern Alaska. However, he could not have considered Dry Strait a viable passage, and although there is nothing in his leaked information to the effect, there can be little doubt that he would have continued his explorations through Sumner Strait and discovered broad Chatham Strait leading northward.

Especially compelling is the evidence that Drake gave the name Nova Albion to Vancouver Island and chose a site on its sheltered eastern coastal plain for the future colony. To this may be added the obvious. Certainly he would have found the climate in Georgia Strait noticeably milder than anywhere else on this northern coast. And there would be a natural delight in finding a large island with an abundance of resources and a climate like England herself, and in the same latitude. Contrast this with the alternative of founding a colony on the rugged coast which he subsequently found south of Cape Flattery, where the anchorage would be exposed to seasonal storms and more easily detected by the Spanish, and there really is no question what his preference would have been.

The proposal drafted soon after his return for a new company of adventurers to exploit his "late notable discovery" leaves no room for doubt that it was in fact Drake's 'dream' to command the new enterprise from Nova Albion as Zelia Nuttall first suggested. And from the size of force he proposed to take with him it is obvious that the focus of the venture was the seizing of more Spanish treasure. Undoubtedly the aspect which appealed most to Drake was that he would be far removed from England and able to operate without having to obtain permission for every initiative. But Elizabeth was not prepared to approve such an enterprise as long as she could avoid war with Spain, and then when war became unavoidable she would not let him go for fear of a Spanish invasion while her most able naval commander was far away in the Pacific. Thus she kept him on a short leash and he was obliged to watch in growing frustration as one expedition after another failed to complete the discovery of the passage.

That Drake remained convinced that he had found the Strait of Anian in spite of his little ships not returning is evident in the involvement of his relations and other veterans of the voyage in the followup expedition of Fenton, and also in the final attempt by Richard Hawkins. And from his efforts in his commemorative maps and leaked information to leave clues to his northern exploit there can be no doubt that the achievement he most wanted to be remembered for was this voyage to the farthest corner of the globe to discover the Strait. However, the continuing insistence of Elizabeth's officials on secrecy around his strategically vital discovery deprived him of that credit. Allowing that he submitted his account to Elizabeth herself and that Molyneux's suppressed globe was eventually redated to the year of her death, it is difficult to avoid the conclusion that she was the chief obstacle to him publishing his story of the voyage.

For Drake to have seen his great reconnaissance as the highlight of his life's adventures is completely understandable. This was a singular display of navigation, leadership, improvisation and sheer tenacity on a scale which was simply magnificent. Indeed, for those who are familiar with the European voyages to this northwest coast of America in the 18th century, it is immediately obvious that Drake's feat of exploration eclipses any achieved in that day. Considering the circumstances under which he had to perform, sailing in an unimaginably crowded little ship and with only the crudest of instruments, some 18,000 miles through uncharted Magellan's Strait and along hostile coasts, even reaching these far distant shores was an extraordinary accomplishment in itself. But then on top of that to have gained in only a few weeks a comprehension of this labyrinthine coast which would not be equalled until years after its rediscovery two centuries later was a truly remarkable achievement. And finally, to then sail another 20,000 miles to reach home and yet lose only one man out of sixty on that leg of this great odyssey was yet another extraordinary feat. Beyond any question, Sir Francis Drake's secret voyage to the northwest coast of America must be regarded as one of the greatest in the history of global exploration.

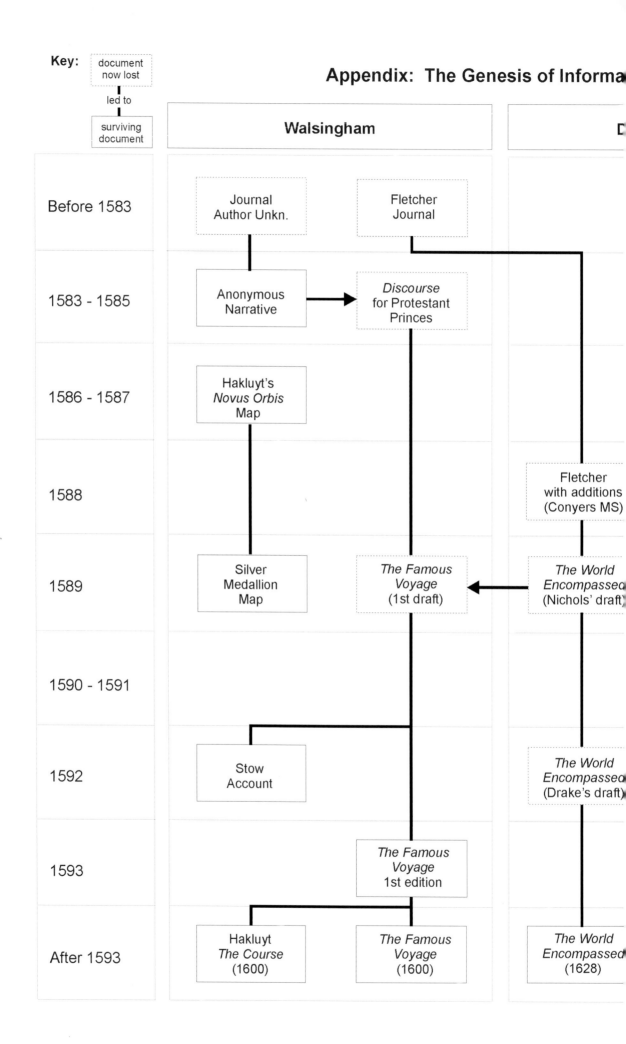

Key:

document now lost

led to

surviving document

Appendix: The Genesis of Informa[tion]

Walsingham

D[rake]

	Walsingham		D...
Before 1583	Journal Author Unkn.	Fletcher Journal	
1583 - 1585	Anonymous Narrative →	*Discourse* for Protestant Princes	
1586 - 1587	Hakluyt's *Novus Orbis* Map		
1588			Fletcher with additions (Conyers MS)
1589	Silver Medallion Map	*The Famous Voyage* (1st draft) ←	*The World Encompassed* (Nichols' draft)
1590 - 1591			
1592	Stow Account		*The World Encompassed* (Drake's draft)
1593		*The Famous Voyage* 1st edition	
After 1593	Hakluyt *The Course* (1600)	*The Famous Voyage* (1600)	*The World Encompassed* (1628)

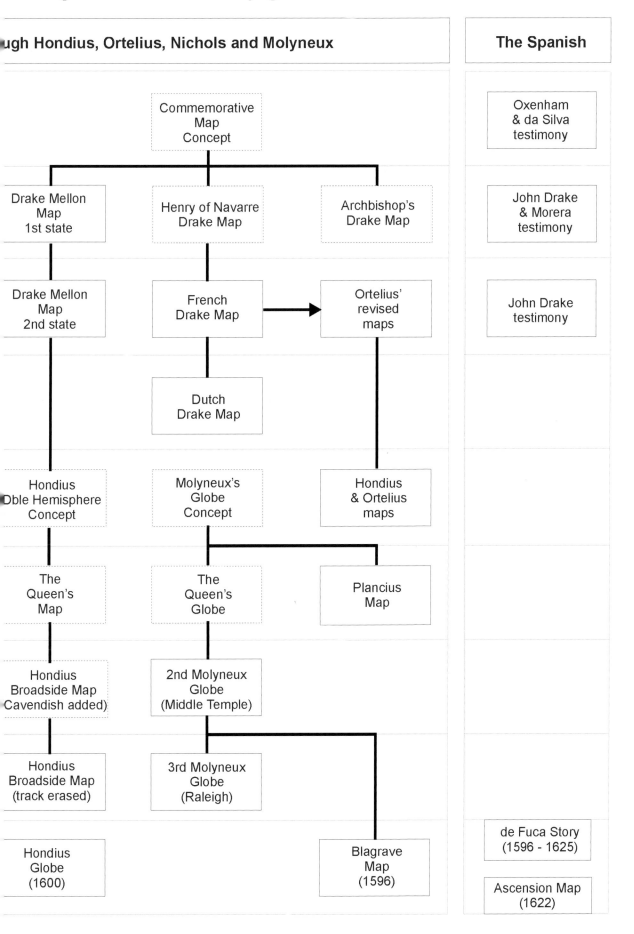

ugh Hondius, Ortelius, Nichols and Molyneux

The Spanish

Commemorative
Map
Concept

Oxenham
& da Silva
testimony

Drake Mellon
Map
1st state

Henry of Navarre
Drake Map

Archbishop's
Drake Map

John Drake
& Morera
testimony

Drake Mellon
Map
2nd state

French
Drake Map

Ortelius'
revised
maps

John Drake
testimony

Dutch
Drake Map

Hondius
Dble Hemisphere
Concept

Molyneux's
Globe
Concept

Hondius
& Ortelius
maps

The
Queen's
Map

The
Queen's
Globe

Plancius
Map

Hondius
Broadside Map
(Cavendish added)

2nd Molyneux
Globe
(Middle Temple)

Hondius
Broadside Map
(track erased)

3rd Molyneux
Globe
(Raleigh)

de Fuca Story
(1596 - 1625)

Hondius
Globe
(1600)

Blagrave
Map
(1596)

Ascension Map
(1622)

Notes

INTRODUCTION • An Enduring Mystery

1   Published by Drake's nephew and namesake, London 1628. I am indebted to Helen Wallis, *The Cartography of Drake's Voyage*, for the idea of opening with this quotation.

2.   Ibid., p. 121-122, 133-137

3.   Hakluyt, *The Principall Navigations,* 1589

4.   Exactly when "The Famous Voyage" was released has never been established. Quinn and Skelton (xxii – xxiv) suggest that the account was made available in early 1590, but Kelsey (p. 178) argues that it may not have been distributed until as late as 1596. Of the 111 surviving copies of *Principall Navigations* enumerated by Payne, 88 contain these socalled "Drake leaves".

5.   Hakluyt, *The Principal Navigations,* 1600

6.   Hanna, *Lost Harbour*, recounts the history of the California anchorage debate and provides a detailed comparison of the arguments for the supposed anchorages.

7.   Ibid., p. 66-71. When the explorer Cermeño anchored in the bay in 1595, his ship was driven ashore by a gale and wrecked. Moreover, although he spent several weeks in the bay, the account of Cermeño's stay does not mention him discovering any evidence of an earlier visit there by Europeans. Yet the remnants of Drake's fortified camp surely would still have been visible after just sixteen years, and the Indians almost certainly would have possessed some articles left by Drake if he had in fact been there. In 1792 Captain George Vancouver commented that the bay offered "little shelter or security".

8.   Nuttall, *New Light on Drake*, p. xxx-xlii

9.   Ibid., p. xxxvii, liv-lvi

10.   Wagner, *Drake's Voyage*

11.   Ibid., p. 19 - 25, 149 - 151

12.   Taylor, *Tudor Geography*

13.   Bishop, *Drake's Course in the North Pacific*

14.   Hanna, *Lost Harbour*, p. 242-262

15.   Ibid., p. 66-82

16.   Ibid., p. 255-256

17.   Quinn, *Early Accounts of the Famous Voyage*

18.   Wallis, *The Cartography of Drake's Voyage*

19.   Ward, *Drake and the Oregon Coast*; *Lost Harbour Found*; and *Drake Maps*

CHAPTER ONE • A Strategically Vital Quest

1.   Quinn, *The Context of early English Northwest Exploration*. Two of the ships were trapped by ice and the crews froze to death.

2.   Taylor, *Tudor Geography*, p. 111

3.   Gilbert, *A Discourse of a Discoverie for a New Passage to Cataia*, circulated in manuscript in 1566 and then printed in 1576

4.   McDermott, *The Company of Cathay*, p. 149-150

5.   BL Lansdowne MS 100, fols. 52 - 54

6.   Taylor, *Tudor Geography*; Sherman, *John Dee's Role*

7.   Sherman, *John Dee's Role*

8.   McDermott, *The Company of Cathay*, p. 157-165

9.   Settle, *A true reporte,* reprinted by Hakluyt in *Principall Navigations*, 1589 (Quinn and Skelton 1965), p.622 – 630

10.   Symons, *Meta Incognita*, p. xxix

11.   Allaire and Hogarth, *Martin Frobisher, the Spaniards and a Sixteenth-Century Northern Spy*

12.   Ibid.

13.   Settle, *A True reporte* (see note 9 above)

14.   Best, *A True Discourse*

15.   Ibid.

16.   Ibid.

17.   Symons, *Meta Incognita*, p. xx

18.   Taylor, *Tudor Geography*, p. 113-119

19.   Ibid., p. 114

20.   Ibid., p. 117, quoting from Dee, *General and Rare Memorials*, 1577

21.   Ibid., p. 114

22.   Ibid., p. 117

23.   Ibid., p. 116, transcribed from BL Cotton MS Vitellius C. vii, ff 178ᵇ, 179. A few words in this passage had to be interpolated because the margins of the document have been burned. None of the interpolations are in dispute. As for Dee's reference to Spanish attempts to discover the Strait 'by land and by sea', the only voyage which is recorded prior to this date which may have had this purpose is that of Juan Rodriguez Cabrillo, who is believed to have reached somewhere between latitudes 40° and 43° when he sailed north from New Spain in 1542.

24.   Ibid.

25.   Kelsey, *The Queen's Pirate*, p. 81, citing PRO SP Domestic, 12/114, item 44, fol. 84

26.   Ibid., p. 83, citing PRO HCA, 25/1, part II. Kelsey also notes that a ship named *Pelican* is listed in another document dated 6 February 1576 (1575), and speculates that this was Drake's new ship, actually completed in 1574. However, a name such as *Pelican* must have been fairly common, and notably Drake's application for the bounty in July 1577 gives the name *Pellican of Plymouthe* for his new ship.

27.   BL Cotton MS Otho E. VIII, fols. 8-9

28.   Ibid.

CHAPTER TWO • Early Accounts of the Northern Voyage

1.   Nuttall, *New Light on Drake* contains the most extensive set of documents. Several others are reprinted in Wagner, *Drake's Voyage*

2.   Ibid., p. 5-12

3.   Ibid., p. 10

4.   Ibid., p. 10

5.   Wagner, *Drake's Voyage*, p. 349

6.   Kelsey, *The Queen's Pirate*, p. 208, citing BL Lansdowne MS 100, no. 2, fols. 71-73v

7.   Ibid., p. 208, citing Mendoza to King Philip, 10 June 1579, AGI Patronato 265, ramo 28

8.   Mendoza to Gabriel de Zayas, 8 September 1579, in Hume, *Calendar of Letters and State Papers*, Vol. II, p. 694-695

9.   Kelsey, *The Queen's Pirate*, p. 209, citing Mendoza to King Philip, 28 December 1579, CDIE, 91:445

10.   Ibid., p. 210, citing Mendoza to King Philip, 20 February 1580, CDIE, 91:452-453

11.   Wallis, *The Cartography of Drake's Voyage*, p. 121, 133, quoting from Mendoza to King Philip, 16 October 1580, BL Additional MS 28420, fol. 30

12.   Nuttall, *New Light on Drake*, p. 430

13.   Wagner, *Drake's Voyage*, p. 214, citing PRO, SP Domestic, Elizabeth CXLIV

14.   Ibid., citing Mendoza, 15 January 1581, CSP, Vol. III, no. 65

15.   Ibid., p. 213, citing Mendoza, CSP, Vol. III, no. 61

16.   Wallis, *The Cartography of Drake's Voyage*, p. 134, quoting from Mendoza, 6 April 1581, CSP, Vol. III, no. 77

17.   Wagner, *Drake's Voyage*, p. 219, citing Mendoza, 9 February 1582, CSP, Vol. III, no. 211

18.   Ibid., p. 445 - 446, transcribed from BL Otho MS E VIII fol. 127

19.   Taylor, *The Troublesome Voyage*, p.50-59, reprinted from Hakluyt, *Principall Navigations*, 1589

20.   Item 10 of Fenton's instructions, Ibid., p.54.   Notably, these instructions are found only in *Principall Navigations* (1589), from which Hakluyt was obliged to omit his account of Drake's voyage. Hakluyt was working for Walsingham at the time and it is likely that Fenton's instructions were carefully edited before publication.

21.   Wagner, *Drake's Voyage,* p. 218

22.   Wallis, ed., *Sir Francis Drake, An Exhibition*, p. 22

23.   Taylor, *The Troublesome Voyage of Captain Edward Fenton*

24.   Donno, *An Elizabethan in 1582*

25.   Ibid., p. 208-209

26.   Ibid., p. 92-93

27.   Taylor, *A Regiment for the Sea*, p. 17, 238-240

28.   Taylor, *The Troublesome Voyage*, p. xxix

29.   AGI Patronato 266, ramo 49, fol. 49

30.   Ibid., ramo 54, fol. 8

31.   Wagner, *Drake's Voyage*, p. 333-334, translated from Herrera, *Historia General de Mundo*

32.   BL Harley MS 280, fols. 83 - 90 and the related Memoranda, fols. 81 - 82.   Transcribed by Vaux in *The World Encompassed* (1584)

33.   The passages which are crossed out contain complaints against Drake by one or more members of his crew.

34.   Wagner, *Drake's Voyage*, p. 243-244; see also Quinn, *Early Accounts*, p. 40

35.   BL Harley MS 280, f. 87-v

36.   This was first noticed by Bob Ward, who drew it to my attention in February 1996 because of my interest in the question of Drake's northern reach. Ward thought that the original entry might have been 50°. I responded that the numerals 48 appeared to be written over 53. Then I wrote to the British Library who kindly undertook to examine and photograph the numerals for me utilizing the Library's *Video Spectral Comparator*.

37.   Wallis, *The Cartography of Drake's Voyage*, p. 133

38.   Ibid., p. 123

39.   Ibid., p. 121-129

40.   Ibid., p. 122-123

41.   Ibid., p. 132

CHAPTER THREE • Islands of Good Land

1.   Williamson, *Sir John Hawkins*, p. 411, citing BL Landsdowne MS 49, fols. 9-10

2.   Ibid.

3.   Corbett, *Drake and the Tudor Navy*, Vol. II, p. 9-10

4.   Parks, *Richard Hakluyt and the English Voyages*, Chapter 8; and *Hakluyt's Mission in France, 1583-1588*

5.   Wallis, *The Cartography of Drake's Voyage*, p. 139, quoting from CSP, Foreign, Elizabeth, Vol. XIX, p. 18

6.   Ibid., p. 123, citing BL Harley MS 376, fol. 5. Henry of Navarre also wrote directly to Drake. PRO SP 78/3 fols. 161-162; CSP France, 1584-85, 334-335

7.   Ibid., p. 139, citing BN, MS Français 15454, fol. 133

8.   Parks, *Richard Hakluyt and the English Voyages*, Chapter 8; Quinn and Skelton, *Principall Navigations*, p. xvii

9.   Wallis, *The Cartography of Drake's Voyage*, p. 161 n.5, citing CSP, Foreign, September 1585 - May 1596, Vol. XX, p. 136. The note is in Lord Burghley's hand, and the reference to Drake's 'first voyage' undoubtedly refers to the one preceding his 1585 Caribbean expedition, i.e. his voyage around the world, as the cautious Burghley certainly would not have supported sending an account of Drake's earlier, piratical voyages to any foreign prince.

10.   Nuttall, *New Light on Drake*, p. xxvii

11.   Wallis, *The Cartography of Drake's Voyage*, p. 143

12.   Wagner, *Drake's Voyage*, p. 430

13.   Sprent, *Two Contemporary Maps*, argues that the portrait of Drake predates 1586 and therefore the map most probably was engraved in 1585 or earlier. However, while I agree that the map was drawn in 1585 (not earlier), I am inclined to Wagner's argument that the Nivelle watermark on the paper dates from the early 17th century, and that van Sype engraved the map in the latter period for inclusion in the French edition of Hakluyt's account.

14.   Preserved at the New York Public Library, Department of Rare Books

CHAPTER FOUR • Leaked Information

1.   Wallis, *The Cartography of Drake's Voyage*, p. 136-137, citing Krause, *Sir Francis Drake*, p. 86. Ortelius would of course have written to Dr. Dee in the hope of obtaining some information, and he is also known to have corresponded from time to time with Richard Hakluyt and John Camden. Reinhartz (1998). It is even possible that Hakluyt sent Ortelius the copy of Henry of Navarre's map from Paris. Another possible link is Ortelius' nephew, Emanuel van Meteren, who was a longtime resident of London and well-acquainted with the Hakluyts.

2.   The placement of this 'river of the straits' appears to have been influenced in part by the pre-existing embayment of Ortelius' coastline in that area.

3.   van den Broecke, *Ortelius Atlas Maps*, p. 3, 11; Shirley, *World Maps in the Theatrum*

4.   Wagner, *Cartography of the Northwest Coast of America*, p. 103

5.   The introduction of the Solomon Islands is especially interesting. The Spanish were very secretive about the islands. The information appears to have come from their co-discoverer Pedro Sarmiento de Gamboa after he was captured and brought to London by one of Raleigh's ships in 1586. Wallis, *The First English Globe*, p.286

6.   Ibid., p. 145, quoting from the biography of Hondius in the preface to the Mercator-Hondius atlas of 1636

7.   Wallis, *Sir Francis Drake, An Exhibition*, p. 34-35

8.   Wallis, *The Cartography of Drake's Voyage*, p. 139

9.   Hakluyt wrote the dedication of *Decades of the New World* on 22 February, and engraver F.G.S. dedicated the map to Hakluyt on 1 May 1587. Then on 4 May Hakluyt left Paris carrying dispatches for London, where he remained for two or three months. Parks, p. 248 – 249. It therefore appears that he must have obtained the manuscript map which F.G.S. subsequently engraved while he was in England the previous year (February to August 1586), or that Walsingham subsequently sent it to him in Paris.

10.   Wagner, *Drake's Voyage*, p. 407. The map may have been taken from Sarmiento (see note 5 above) or brought back from the Caribbean by Drake the previous July.

11.   Ruggles, *Cartographic Lure of the Northwest Passage*, p. 221-222

12.   Wallis, *The Cartography of Drake's Voyage*, p. 149

13.   Ibid., p. 150

14.   Although Ortelius' *Maris Pacifici* is dated 1589, it was first included in his atlas the following year. van den Broecke, *Ortelius Atlas Maps*, p. 12

15.   It is strange that Wagner, *Cartography of the Northwest Coast*, p. 71-75, lists all of these new toponyms found on Ortelius' maps and puzzles over their origin, but in spite of his voluminous work on Drake's voyage, fails or refuses to recognize their connection to Drake. To my knowledge, the first person to suggest a possible connection was Bob Ward. The work of integrating the nomenclatures and matching them to the coast as presented herein, however, is my own.

16.   Wallis, *The First English Globe*; *Further Light on the Molyneux Globes*

17.   Wallis, *Sir Francis Drake, An Exhibition*, p. 80-81

18.   Plancius' 1590 map, a double hemisphere design, was produced for insertion in a new Bible. As with the new nomenclature on the maps of Ortelius, Wagner overlooks the possible link to Drake and characterizes Plancius' toponyms, like his coastline, as being purely imaginary. Wagner, *Cartography of the Northwest Coast*, p. 75, 97-102.

19.   Wagner, *Cartography of the Northwest Coast*, p. 101

20.   Ibid., p. 103-106. In spite of Hondius' residency in England and his direct involvement in the cartography of Drake's voyage, Wagner fails to recognize the obvious likelihood of Hondius' northern toponyms having originated with Drake.

CHAPTER FIVE • 'That posterity be not deprived'

1.   Dyke, *The Finance of a 16th Century Navigator*, p. 111

2.   Hakluyt, *Principall Navigations*, 1600, Vol. III

3.   Ibid., p. 819

4.   Cavendish's doubt is noted on Hondius' Broadside map. See also Wallis, *The Cartography of Drake's Voyage*, p. 146, 151-153

5.   Quinn and Skelton, *Principall Navigations*, p. xx

6.   Quinn, *Early Accounts of the Famous Voyage*

7.   There is no evidence that Drake's nephew edited or added anything to the narrative beyond the introductory paragraphs.

8.   Quinn, *Early Accounts of the Famous* Voyage, p. 38, 45-46. Beyond what Quinn relates, nothing further is known of Fletcher after the voyage.

9.   Conyers, BL Sloane MS 61, transcribed in Penzer, *The World Encompassed*, p. 87 - 142

10.   Ibid., p. 137

11.   Quinn, *Early Accounts of the Famous Voyage*, p. 35-36

12.   Ibid., p. 34

13.   Kelsey, *The Queen's Pirate*, p. 178

14.   Crinò and Wallis, *New Researches on the Molyneux Globes*, p. 14

15.   Ibid.

16.   Wagner, *Cartography of the Northwest Coast*, p. 83

17.   Blundeville, *His Exercises*, reprinted in Wagner, *Drake's Voyage*, p. 311-313

18.   Wallis, *The First English Globe*, p. 281

19.   Verbal communications with Sylvia Sumira, who did extensive restoration work on Raleigh's globe, and with Niki Ingram, Manager of Collections, Petworth House, where the globe is preserved.

20.   Wallis, *Further Light on the Molyneux Globes* p. 307

21.   Wallis, *The First English* Globe, p. 281. The changes relate to the discoveries of Barents on his third voyage (1596), and involved only the re-engraving of two of the globe's gores in the region of Novaya Zemlya.

22.   Crashaw served the Middle Temple from 1605 until 1613.

23.   Wallis, *The First English Globe*, p. 281. On Raleigh's globe the tracks of Drake and Cavendish are usually indicated by their initials, S.F.D. and T.C., whereas the Middle Temple globe has their full names. And on Raleigh's globe wherever Cavendish's name is spelled in full, it is *Thomae Candis*, whereas

on the Middle Temple globe it is spelled *Thomae Candyssh*. The latter spelling of Cavendish's name was found on the fragments of gores recovered from under the surface of Raleigh's globe.

24.   Bob Ward was the first to notice the notch in the coastline where Vancouver Island fits.

25.   Stow's account of Drake's voyage, reprinted in Wagner, *Drake's Voyage*, p. 303-305

26.   Whatever Stow proposed to publish about Drake's voyage undoubtedly was subject to scrutiny by an official censor or 'corrector'. See Quinn and Skelton, *Principall Navigations*, p. xx-xxi

27.   Quinn, *Early Accounts of the Famous Voyage*, points out that while the date of Drake's letter to the Queen enclosing the two volumes is 1 January 1592, the English legal year began on 25 March and most probably the actual date of the letter, by our reckoning, would be 1 January 1593.

28.   Drake's letter to Elizabeth is prefixed to *Sir Francis Drake revived*, sig. A3. It appears that Drake must have enclosed *Sir Francis Drake revived* followed by *The World Encompassed* with the letter, and his nephew, finding the letter pinned to the face of the first account, decided that it should be published with it rather than *The World Encompassed*.

29.   The complete account is reprinted in Penzer, *The World Encompassed*.

30.   Kelsey, *The Queen's Pirate*, p. 178-179, argues that "The Famous Voyage" did not appear until sometime after 1592 and probably not before 1596. However, the evidence he cites in support of a date later than 1593 is the fact that two Dutch historians, Jan Huygen van Linschoten and Emanuel van Meteren, appear not to have taken anything from "The Famous Voyage" in their writings dated 1594 and 1595 respectively. The fact that they did not draw from Hakluyt's account is not compelling evidence for Kelsey's conclusion that they were *unable* to do so. There may be other explanations. Notably, both appear to have been serious researchers who were especially interested in previously unpublished material. Conceivably also, Hakluyt's account may have been available only on commercial terms which they were reluctant to meet or circumvent.

31.   I am indebted to Francis Herbert, Curator of Maps, Royal Geographical Society, for translating the Dutch account of Drake's voyage accompanying the Broadside map.

CHAPTER SIX • The Last Glimpses

1.   Williamson, *The Observations of Sir Richard Hawkins*, p. xlix-lll. Hawkins had originally undertaken construction of his ship *Dainty* for the express purpose of a South Sea expedition in late 1588, soon after Cavendish returned from his first voyage and the bark *Content* failed to return via the northwest passage. This suggests a Drake-Hawkins family scheme to regain control of the Pacific enterprise and complete the discovery of the passage themselves. From the fact that Hawkins did not go and Cavendish went out again, however, it appears that Elizabeth may have withheld permission for Hawkins' voyage in favour of John Davis' plan.

2.   Ibid. There can be little doubt that the thinking at the time of Fenton's and Cavendish's voyages was that once the discovery of the northwest passage was complete a major naval force would be sent through the passage to prosecute the Pacific enterprise, and so the hint of a major expedition going out when Hawkins returned supports the inference that his objective was to complete the discovery of the passage.

3.   Hakluyt, "The Course ...", in *Principal Navigations*, 1600, Vol. III, p. 440 - 442

4.   Ward, *Drake's Maps*. This accurate detail of Cape Flattery was first noticed by Ward, and it led him to the conclusion that Drake must have sailed into the Strait of Juan de Fuca. Indeed, to have drawn the cape so accurately Drake had to have been in the strait.

5.   Monson, *Naval Tracts*

6.   Ibid., p. 400

7.   Ibid.

8.   Ibid., p. 434

9.   Ibid.

10.   Ibid.

11.   Beaglehole, *The Journals of Captain James Cook*, p. ccxxi

CHAPTER SEVEN • Tracing Drake's Explorations

1.   Bishop, *Drake's Course in the North Pacific*
2.   Ibid., p. 165
3.   Ibid., p. 164
4.   Oral history related by tribal elders of the Checleset Indian band in the Campbell River, B.C. newspaper, 17 February 1982.
5.   Bradley and Jones, *Climate Since AD 1500*. Although systematic written records of the weather prior to the 19th century are rare, scientists have managed from comparison of those that do exist with studies of tree ring growth, lake and ocean sediments and ice cores to establish that *global average* temperatures in this period ranged as far as 1 to 1½ degrees Celsius (2 to 3° Fahrenheit) below the average for the mid 20th century. To the layman it may seem that such a small difference hardly warrants the term Little Ice Age. However, the global average temperature in the mid 20th century was only about 5°C warmer than at the nadir of the last Ice Age some 20,000 years ago, and so the difference is very significant.

Several papers in *Climate Since A.D. 1500* offer insights on the conditions in the 16th century. The *Russian Chronicles* are a superb record of crop and weather conditions spanning the centuries, and these reveal that around 1525 the incidence of weather extremes began to increase (Borisenkov). Notwithstanding intervals of mild weather, the climate definitely was turning colder. Broadly what was happening was the domes of cold air over the poles were expanding, causing sharper temperature contrasts at the polar weather fronts and deeper accumulations of snow and more protracted winters in the higher latitudes. A corresponding effect was shorter, cooler summers. Ice cores taken in the Russian arctic show that some of the coolest summers in the last 500 years occurred in the 1570's and 1580's (Tarussov).

Also, an *El Niño* event occurred in 1578 (Quinn and Neal), and this may have contributed to the terrible storms which Drake encountered when he emerged from Magellan's Strait. The *La Niña* which often follows an *El Niño* event can bring cooler temperatures and stormier weather as far north as the Gulf of Alaska. Conceivably the onset of a *La Niña* event may have compounded and extended winter on the northwest coast of America in 1579. However, it is inconceivable that there would have been a residual accumulation of snow along the coast of northern California in June as the rejigged accounts of Drake's voyage claim. For this to have occurred in latitude 38°, the coast would have to have been exposed to freezing temperatures for an extended period, not just a freak storm, and this would require temperatures in June which were radically different (some 8°C/14°F colder) than the modern norm. Notably in the most prolonged winter in the modern record for Prince Rupert, latitude 54°, the daily low hovered around the freezing point into May, but 300 miles to the south at Vancouver they remained a little above the norm, with little freezing past the middle of February.
6.   In 1774, when Juan Perez became the first explorer of record to reach Cape Knox, 200 Haida came out to meet him in twenty-one canoes ranging in length up to 40 feet. They were clothed in skins and woven capes, and wore bracelets of copper and iron, the latter no doubt traded down the coast from the Russians, who were established at Kodiak a thousand miles to the northwest. Perez found the Haida eager to trade, offering furs, colourful woven blankets, finely crafted spoons and bowls, and brightly painted wooden boxes in exchange for ribbons, beads, and especially more iron. Subsequent explorers generally were met in the same way, but elsewhere in the Queen Charlottes during the ensuing maritime fur trade the Haida reception sometimes became lethal.
7.   Perez (see also note 6 above) could see the snowcapped mountains extending northward beyond a cape about 50 miles to the northeast, but he was unable to make any headway into Dixon Entrance on account of light winds and the strong current, which set him back every time the tide turned to ebb.
8.   The pinnacle of rock on Cape Chacon takes the form of a perfect cone only when viewed from the southwest approach, through Dixon Entrance.

9.   Verbal communications with several residents, archaeologists and historians in southeastern Alaska.

10.   The gentleman who found these items, Mr. Donald MacDonald, contacted me after reading a newspaper report of my research. He is 78 years of age and lives in a small, remote Alaskan community. He had no knowledge of the references to lead plates in the Drake manuscripts and he is not a publicity-seeker. Another person has independently corroborated his story, and I have passed all of the information on to the appropriate public agencies. The location of the site remains confidential in order to protect its integrity pending a proper archaeological investigation.

11.   On the coast of Africa they landed on 27 December, assembled a pinnace, and then departed on 31 December—a stop of four days.

12.   In his testimony, John Drake says they discovered "five or six islands of good land", undoubtedly meaning large islands capable of sustaining European habitation. Here it is possible to complete their identification. Deciphering of the Dutch Drake map establishes that four of the islands were the Queen Charlottes, seen as one, Prince of Wales Island, Vancouver Island, and the Olympic Peninsula, which evidently was suspected to be an island and probably represents John Drake's "or six". But there are no other large islands in these latitudes and Drake probably would have regarded Dall Island on the west side of Prince of Wales Island as too small and exposed to rate as an island of good land. However, if as suggested he had continued up Chatham Strait and through Fredrick Sound to the southern end of Stephens Passage, he would in all probability have seen the land between Chatham Strait and the Stikine Delta as two more islands—Kuiu Is. and the remainder (actually comprised of Kupreanof Is. and Mitkof Is.)—which were potentially habitable. The present town of Petersburg, Alaska is located on Mitkof Island.

13.   When the explorer Galiano entered nearby Arran Rapids in 1792, the 45 tonne frigate *Sutil* was caught in a whirlpool and spun around three times so quickly that the sailors were dizzy before they broke free. They used oars to fend her off the rocks until she reached a small cove between two sets of rapids, where they anchored. That night, "the violent flow of the waters in the channel caused a horrible roaring and a notable echo, this producing an awe-inspiring situation, so that we had so far met with nothing so terrible".

14.   An estimate based on discussion with Grant Keddie, Curator of Archaeology, Royal British Columbia museum. Unfortunately it is difficult to obtain native oral history for the Comox area because the Pentlatch people were nearly wiped out by disease and northern marauders in the late 18th century. Harris, *Voices of Disaster: Smallpox.*

15.   The area where Drake most likely set up his 'totem pole', no doubt bearing one of his inscribed lead plates, is somewhere along the beach inside Goose Spit, which is now absorbed into the town of Comox and a military depot. Also of interest, there is a native petroglyph on the shore of Baynes Sound which is said to depict a bearded figure wearing a helmet.

16.   Gleeson, *Ozette Woodworking Technology*; Ward, *Drake Maps*. Altogether 28 ferrous bladed and 14 ferrous stained tool hafts were found in the earliest level of the buried dwellings, dating from 440 years before present (1980), plus or minus 90 years. Spectrographic analysis established that all are high carbon steel. There are three basic types: knife blades made from flat plate 3 mm thick, chisel blades made from rectangular stock of varying dimension, and drill bits made of small, square, nail-like pieces. Gleeson hypothesizes that the metal may have come from the wreck of a Japanese junk which drifted across the Pacific. However, no specific metallurgical tests have yet been undertaken comparing these items to articles of a similar type and date manufactured in Japan and England. It is even possible that Drake had his blacksmith set up the forge at one of their landings in response to the demand for such items from the Indians.

17.   Costaggini and Schultz, *Survey of Artifacts at Neahkahnie Mountain.* Local historian Wayne Jenson of the Tillamook County Pioneer Museum deserves to be congratulated for persevering in his investigation of the cairns and for bringing in the American Society of Civil Engineers. The survey may be the most important artifact of Elizabethan science yet found in North America.

18.   Scale drawing of a survey laid out by William Bourne, BL Sloane MS 3651, fol. 65, reproduced in Taylor, *A Regiment for the Sea*, p. xxxi. It appears that Bourne's survey, set up in Kent near Gravesend, was the Elizabethan precursor to the prime meridian at Greenwich. Still to be solved is how his method resulted in the arrangement of these surveys on the ground, but it is very fortunate indeed that we have the cairns and the engineers' report for Neahkahnie to work from. Eventually it should be possible to model the survey on computer and reconstruct Bourne's method.

19.   The master of Fenton's ship was Christopher Hall, who had served as chief pilot on Frobisher's voyages. Kenyon, *Voyages of Martin Frobisher*, p. 138, notes that there are several cairns which were set up by Frobisher (or Hall) on Christopher Hall Island, at the entrance to his 'strait'. And notably also, Drake did not sail from England until two months after Frobisher's return from his 1577 voyage. Conceivably then, one of Hall's tasks on that voyage may have been to set up Bourne's survey and bring back the longitude of the eastern entrance to the passage for Drake to compare with his position in the Pacific. And interestingly, Settle's report on Frobisher's 1577 voyage specifically refers to knowledge of the longitude of his strait, and to them 'piling up stones', although as said in Chapter I these may have been for another purpose. As previously said, at best the results would incorporate a significant factor of error. However, it appears that the lunar distance method did develop some utility, as by 1616 William Baffin's "estimations of longitude based on observations of the moon and laborious calculations were often accurate to within 1°." Lehane, *The Northwest Passage*, p. 60.

20.   Ward, *Lost Harbour Found*

21.   There are a few Indian words recorded in *The World Encompassed*:

Tobâh	an herb
Gnaah	sing (a request)
Hioh	chief or king
Petáh	an edible root

Also, Madox recorded two words and two phrases in his diary after talking to Drake's men (three years after their visit to northwest America):

Cheepe	bread
Hucheė kecharo	sit down
Nocharo mu	touch me not
Hioghe	chief or king

Heizer and Elmsdorf, "Francis Drake's California Anchorage in light of the Indian Language Spoken There", claim, four centuries after the fact, that these few words positively identify the Indians at the careenage as being the Coast Miwok tribe of the San Francisco Bay area. Far more convincing is the description of the houses, which unmistakably were of the log and earth-covered *kickwilli* type. No such house type has been found in the San Francisco Bay area. Notably, the report of Spanish explorer Cermeño's stay at Drake's Bay, north of San Francisco, in November-December 1595 states that the Miwok dwelled in "pits made in the sand and covered with grass, in the manner of the chichimecos Indians" (of Mexico).

22.   Bob Ward deserves to be congratulated for his twenty year-long effort to call attention to Whale Cove as the site of Drake's careenage. The story of his investigation, beyond what he has already published, should properly be told by Ward himself.

CHAPTER EIGHT • An Old Sailors Yarn

1.   Lok, *A Note ... touching the Strait of Sea, commonly called Fretum Anian*, Samuel Purchas, *Purchas, His Pilgrimes* (reprint, 1905), p. 415 - 421

2.   Ibid.

3.   Ibid.

4.   Ibid.

5.   Richard Hakluyt, to whom Lok wrote in 1596 relating de Fuca's story, uncharacteristically did not include anything about it in his second edition of *Principall Navigations*. It was finally published in 1625 by Samuel Purchas, who came into possession of Hakluyt's papers after his death. It is possible then that Hakluyt had contemplated publishing de Fuca's story and had edited it for the purpose, including perhaps altering the latitude of de Fuca's strait to "betweene 47 and 48 degrees", and then it had been decided that nothing should be published.

6.   In the account of Cavendish's voyage by 'NH' (PN, 1589) the captured Greek pilot is not named. Then in the account by Pretty (PN, 1600) he is mentioned and given the name 'George'. However, this name appears three times in the space of a few lines. Just prior to mentioning the capture of the Greek, the account states "then we burned them all saving one Barke which wee kept, and named it the George, because we took her on Saint George his day". It seems very likely that the Greek was inadvertently misnamed by Hakluyt in the process of redrafting the account, and that he was actually the same 'Juan' or 'John the Greek' whom Drake captured in the same area of the coast eight years previous. De Fuca must have had a lot of colourful stories to tell. See also Wagner, *Drake's Voyage*, p. 477 - 478.

7.   Wagner, *Spanish Voyages*, p. 169

8.   The actual purpose of Vizcaino's first voyage (1594) was to establish a fortified settlement on the Baja Peninsula of Mexico, then known as Nueva Andalusia, to guard the area where Cavendish had waited to intercept the Manila galleon. There was some concern at the time that the English might have discovered a seapassage leading northward from the Gulf of California, and so Vizcaino's mission does appear to be a consequence of Morera's story. After exploring some distance northward in the Gulf and then landing in Baja Sur, Vizcaino had to cut the voyage short on account of a mutiny against the captain of the soldiers. From his knowledge of this incident, it appears that de Fuca probably served as Vizcaino's pilot, but in telling his story to Lok moved the date of the expedition back in time to leave room for his fictitious voyage, which he said occurred in 1592.

9.   Wagner, *Spanish Voyages*, p. 171, 173, 176. Vizcaino led a second expedition into the Gulf of California in May 1596, the month following de Fuca's meetings with Lok in Venice, and then in 1602 he set out to explore the Pacific coast of California, and Father Ascension accompanied him on this last voyage.

10.   Salmeron, *Relaciones*, p. 197 - 199, translated in *Land of Sunshine*, February 1900, and reprinted in Hanna, *Lost Harbour*, p. 387 - 388. In Salmeron's relation he gives the pilot's name as Morena.

11.   After Drake arrived at Guatulco the Alcalde of the town, Gaspar de Vargas, dashed off a letter to the Viceroy of New Spain in which he relates: "a third time, I came back at midnight to see if I could find out who they were, and all that I could discover was that their pilot, according to what the crew of the Juan de Madrid found, was called Morera". Reprinted in Wagner, *Drake's Voyage*, p. 380.

12.   Salmeron, *Relaciones* (see note 10 above)

13.   Herrera, *Descriptis Indae Occidentalis*, 1622. The map is featured on the title page of the book. Around this same date variations on Ascension's map began to be printed in the Netherlands and England as well.

14.   Ward, *Drake and The Oregon Coast*, first raised the possibility that the stories of de Fuca and Morera were somehow related.

15.   Nuttall, *New Light on Drake*, p. 420 - 428; Hanna, *Lost Harbour*, p. 54 - 65. Estimates of the size of Drake's company by his released captives range from 71 to 72 (estimated by Nicholas Jorge) to 86 or 87. Apart from Jorge's estimate, all the others place the number at 80 or more.

16.   John Drake testified that apart from three liberated slaves—the black woman Maria and two black men—they departed Guatulco with "men of their own nation only", by which presumably he meant loyal to the English cause. In point of fact there appear to have been several nationalities among the men who returned to England with Drake. In any case, John Drake said they then reduced the ship's company to 60 men in the Moluccas (not including the three black people, who were left at the 'Island of Crabs', near Celebes)—but there is no other evidence that he did so, and this assertion appears to be a fabrication to cover for the fact that Drake left the missing men on the northwest coast of America.

17.   In Ascension's map the meridians are laid out at 15° intervals.

18.   Here it is important to emphasize that the *Anonymous Narrative* is the only surviving manuscript account of Drake's Pacific voyage, and was written well before the much-edited published accounts. Apart from the altered numerals '48' and some crossing out of passages which are critical of Drake, there is no sign of tampering with any of the information contained in it. It is quite evident that the information, although compressed in the case of Drake's northern voyage, was copied directly from a journal or deposition obtained from one or more of Drake's men shortly after their return from the Pacific. Therefore, it must be regarded as the most reliable source for the dates of Drake's departure from the careenage and his first landfall across the Pacific. This means that the published accounts of Drake's voyage from northwest America to England have been padded with two months of fiction to make up the difference. Still, considering that from Cape St. Lucas on 20 November, Cavendish reached Plymouth on 9 September following, the time left to Drake between his initial landfall in the western Pacific at the end of November and his arrival at Plymouth on 26 September following seems quite reasonable.

19.   Ironically it was here at Coos Bay that the Drake Navigators Guild of San Francisco, advocates for Drake's Bay as the site of the careenage and Nova Albion, set up a plaque marking Drake's northernmost reach.

20.   Relation of Pedro Sarmiento de Gamboa, reprinted in Wagner, *Drake's Voyage*, p. 395. After their discover of the Solomon Islands in 1567, Sarmiento and Mendaña followed Urdaneta's route from Manila to the Californias, and Sarmiento undoubtedly was familiar with the Spanish charts of the Californias.

21.   An obvious question then, is what became of the little Spanish bark and the pinnace? Notably Whale Cove is exposed to the southwest gales which lash the Oregon coast through the winter months, and these mariners would have been alert to that eventuality. But they could not abandon the cove because they might miss their rescuers. Therefore they would have been obliged to leave the vessels in a better place and hope that they survived the elements and the Indians. A few miles north of Whale Cove is the Salmon River, and there is a story, which I have been unable to substantiate, that there is an old wreck here, possibly lying under a more recent wreck in the mouth of the river. According to the story, someone retrieved a piece of the old wreck and found that it was Central American wood, but they were unable to obtain a permit to excavate the vessel. If so, perhaps this is just as well until archaeologists become organized around this whole subject.

22.   In this period England appears to have attracted into her service quite a few renegade Portuguese mariners, the pilot Simon Fernandes (or Ferdinando) who later accompanied Fenton being another.

23.   Hanna, *Lost Harbour*, p. 59

24.   There is also evidence that a group of Elizabethan mariners became stranded further south, near present Santa Barbara. On his 1602 voyage Vizcaino reported the wreck of a bark on Catalina Island and noted that a number of the Indian children on the island were "white and blonde". Then on the mainland opposite, the Indians told him by signs that there were men inland from there who had beards and weapons like the Spaniards. Also, I am told that some years ago four Elizabethan cannons were discovered in an estuary near Santa Barbara. I am unaware whether anyone has drawn the connection, but it seems likely that all of this relates to Cavendish's missing bark, the *Content*. It appears that the wreck was sufficiently intact for her crew to retrieve the cannons, and possible their cargo of treasure as well, and ferry them across to the mainland in the ship's launch. That was 15 years before Vizcaino's observations however, and from the Indians' story it appears that the sailors must have taken up residence somewhere behind the Santa Barbara mountains. Perhaps something more will be found someday.

Bibliography

Manuscripts

British Library:
> *Additional Manuscript 28420, fol.* 30 (Mendoza to King Philip, 16 October 1580)
> *Cotton, Otho E. VIII, fols. 8 - 9*   (planning of Drake's Voyage)
> *Harley 280, fols. 81 - 90* (the Anonymous Narrative and related memoranda)
> *Lansdowne 100, fols. 52 - 54* (Grenville's proposal to discover the Strait of Anian)
> *Sloane 3651, fol. 65*   (plan of Bourne's survey at Gravesend)

Archivo General de Indias, Seville:
> *Patronato 266, ramo 49, fol. 49 and ramo 54, fol. 8* (John Drake's testimony to the Inquisition)

Contemporary Printed Works

Best, George. *A True Discourse of the late Voyages of Discoverie for finding of a Passage to Cathaya by the North-west under the conduct of Martin Frobisher, General.* London 1578. Reprinted by Collinson, 1867

Gilbert, Sir Humphrey. *A Discourse of a Discoverie for a new passage to Cataia.* London, 1576

Hakluyt, Richard. *Diverse voyages touching the discoverie of America, and the Ilands adiacent.* London, 1582. Reprinted, Hakluyt Society, London, 1850

_____. *The Principall Navigations Voiages and Discoveries of the English Nation.* London 1589. Facsimile edition, Hakluyt Society, Cambridge, 1965

_____.*The Voyages, Navigations, Trafiques, and Discoveries of the English Nation.* London, 1600. (also cited as *Principall Navigations*, 1600). Reprinted, Hakluyt Society, London, 1903 - 1905

Monson, Sir William. "Sir William Monson's Naval Tracts" in Awnsham Churchill, *A Collection of Voyages and Travels*, 8 vols., London 1704

Purchas, Samuel. *Purchas, His Pilgrimes.* London, 1625. Reprinted, Glasgow, 1905 - 1907

Books, Articles and Papers

Allaire, Bernard, and Donald Hogarth. "Martin Frobisher, the Spaniards and a Sixteenth Century Northern Spy", in Symons, ed. *Meta Incognita*

Beaglehole, John C. *The Journals of Captain James Cook on His Voyages of Discovery: The Voyage of the Resolution and Discovery, 1776 - 1780.* Cambridge, 1967

Bishop, R.P. "Drake's Course in the North Pacific", *British Columbia Historical Quarterly*, July 1939

Boyd, Robert T. "Demographic History, 1774 - 1874", Vol. 7, *Northwest Coast Handbook of North American Indians*, Smithsonian Institute, 1990

Bradley, R.G., and P.D. Jones eds. *Climate Since A.D. 1500.* London, 1992

Corbett, Julian S. *Drake and the Tudor Navy*, 2 vols. London, 1898

Costaggini, P.A. and R.J. Schultz. *Survey of Artifacts at Neahkahnie Mountain* (unpubl. paper), Oregon State U., 1980

Crinò, Anna Maria, and Helen Wallis. "New Researches on the Molyneux Globes", *Der Globusfreund*, Wien, 1987

Davidson, George. "Francis Drake on the Northwest Coast of America in the Year 1579". *Geographical Society of the Pacific*, Vol. V., Series II, San Francisco, 1908

Donno, Elizabeth S. *An Elizabethan in 1582, the Diary of Richard Madox, Fellow of All Souls.* Hakluyt Society, London, 1976

Dyke, Gwenyth. "The Finance of a 16th Century Navigator, Thomas Cavendish of Trimley in Sussex", *The Mariner's Mirror*, Cambridge, February 1958

Eliott-Drake, Lady Elizabeth Fuller. *The Family and Heirs of Sir Francis Drake*, 2 vols. London, 1911

Gleeson, Paul F. *Ozette Woodworking Technology*, Laboratory of Archaeology and History, Washington State University, 1980

Hanna, Warren L. *Lost Harbour: The Controversy Over Drake's California Anchorage.* Berkeley, 1979

Harris, Cole. "Voices of Disaster: Smallpox around the Strait of Georgia in 1782", in *Ethnohistory*, American Society for Ethnohistory, 1974

Heizer, Robert F. and William W. Elmendorf. "Francis Drake's California Anchorage in the Light of the Language Spoken There". *Pacific Historical Review*, Vol. XI, 1942

Hibbert, Christopher. *The Virgin Queen.* London, 1990

House, Derek. "The Lunar-Distance Method of Measuring Longitude", in William J.H. Andrews, *The Quest for Longitude*, Cambridge, Mass., 1996

Howay, F.W. "Early Navigation of the Straits of Juan de Fuca", *Oregon Historical Review*, 1911
_____. "The Spanish Discovery of B.C. in 1774", *Canadian Historical Association*, Annual Report, Ottawa, 1923

Hume, Martin A.S., ed. *Calendar of Letters and State Papers Relating to English Affairs Preserved Principally in the Archives of Simancas.* Vols. 2 – 4. *Elizabeth, 1568 - 1603.* London: Her Majesty's Stationery Office, 1868 - 99

Jane, Cecil. transl. *A Spanish Voyage to Vancouver (Island) and the northwest coast of America*

Keddie, Grant. "The Question of Asiatic Objects on the North Pacific Coast of America", in *Contributions to Human History*, Royal British Columbia Museum, 1990

Kelsey, Harry. *Sir Francis Drake, The Queen's Pirate.* New Haven, 1998

Kendrick, John. *The Men with Wooden Feet: The Spanish Exploration of the Pacific Northwest.* Toronto, 1986

Kenyon, W.A. *Tokens of Possession: The Northern Voyages of Martin Frobisher.* Royal Ontario Museum, Toronto, 1975

Krause, Hans P. *Sir Francis Drake, A Pictorial Biography.* Amsterdam, 1970

Lamb, W. Kaye, ed. *The Voyage of George Vancouver.* Hakluyt Society, London, 1984

Lehane, Brendan. *The Northwest Passage.* Virginia, 1981

McDermott, James. "The Company of Cathay: the Financing and Organization of the Frobisher Voyages", in Symons, ed. *Meta Incognita*

McDermott, James, and David W. Waters, "Cathay and the Way Thither: the Navigation of the Frobisher Voyages", in Symons, ed. *Meta Incognita*

Mason, A.E.W. *The Life of Francis Drake.* London, 1941

Mathes, W.M. *Vizcaino and Spanish Expansion in the Pacific Ocean.* San Francisco, 1968

Morison, Samuel Eliot. *The Great Explorers: The European Discovery of America.* New York, 1978

Nuttall, Zelia. *New Light on Drake*, Hakluyt Society, 1914

Parker, Geoffrey. *The Grand Strategy of Philip II.* New Haven, 1998

Parks, George B. *Richard Hakluyt and the English Voyages.* New York, 1928
_____. "Hakluyt's Mission in France, 1583 - 1588". *Washington University Studies*, No. 9, 165 - 184, St. Louis

Payne, Anthony. *Richard Hakluyt And His Books.* Annual Talk, Hakluyt Society, 1996

Penzer, N.M. *The World Encompassed and Analagous Contemporary Documents*. London, 1926. Reprint, Amsterdam, 1971

Quinn, David B. *The Hakluyt Handbook*, 2 vols. Hakluyt Society, London, 1974

_____, ed. *The Last Voyage of Thomas Cavendish, 1591 - 1592*. Chicago, 1975

_____. "Early Accounts of the Famous Voyage", in Thrower, ed. *Sir Francis Drake*

_____. *Sir Francis Drake as Seen by His Contemporaries*. John Carter Brown Library, 1996

_____. "Frobisher in the Context of early English Northwest Exploration",. in Symons, ed. *Meta Incognita*

Quinn, David B. and R.A. Skelton. *The Principall Navigations, Voiages and Discoveries of the English Nation*, 1589. Facsimile, Hakluyt Society, Cambridge, 1965

Reinhartz, Dennis. "The Americas Revealed in the *Theatrum*", in van den Broecke et al, eds., *Abraham Ortelius*

Rowse, A.L. *Sir Richard Grenville of the Revenge*. London, 1937

Ruggles, Richard I. "The Cartographic Lure of the Northwest Passage: Its Real and Imaginary Geography", in Symons, ed. *Meta Incognita*

Sherman, William H. "John Dee's Role in Martin Frobisher's Northwest Enterprise", in Symons, ed. *Meta Incognita*

Shirley, Rodney. "The World Maps in the *Theatrum*", in van den Broecke et al, eds., *Abraham Ortelius*

Sprent, F.P. *Sir Francis Drake's Voyage Around The World: Two Contemporary Maps*. British Museum, 1927

Sugden, John. *Sir Francis Drake*, New York, 1990

Symons, Thomas H.B., ed. *Meta Incognita: A Discourse of Discovery, Martin Frobisher's Arctic Expeditions, 1576 - 1578*. Canadian Museum of Civilization, Hull, 1999

Taylor, Eva G.R. *Tudor Geography, 1485 - 1582*. London, 1930

_____. "The Missing Draft Project of Drake's Voyage, 1577 - 1580". *Geographical Journal* (75), January 1930

_____. "More Light on Drake", *Mariner's Mirror* (16), April 1930

_____. "Francis Drake and the Pacific: Two Fragments", *Pacific Historical Review*, Vol. 1, no. 2, 1932

_____. *Late Tudor and Early Stuart Geography*. London, 1934

_____, ed. *The Original Writings and Correspondence of the Two Richard Hakluyts*. Hakluyt Society, London, 1935

_____, ed. *The Troublesome Voyage of Captain Edward Fenton, 1582 - 83*. Hakluyt Society, Cambridge, 1959

_____, ed. *A Regiment for the Sea and other writings on Navigation*, Hakluyt Society, Cambridge, 1963

Thomson, George Malcolm. *Sir Francis Drake*. London, 1972

Thrower, Norman J.W., ed. *Sir Francis Drake and the Famous Voyage, 1577 - 1580*. U. of California Press, 1984

van den Broecke, Marcel P.R. *Ortelius Atlas Maps*. Netherlands, 1996

van den Broecke, Marcel P.R., Peter van der Krogt and Peter Meurer, eds.*Abraham Ortelius and the First Atlas: Essay Commemorating the Quadricentennial of his Death, 1598 - 1998*. Netherlands, 1998

Vaux, W.S.W., ed. *The World Encompassed by Sir Francis Drake, Being his Next Voyage to that to Nombre De Dios*. Hakluyt Society, London, 1854

Wagner, Henry R. *Sir Francis Drake's Voyage Around the World, Its Aims and Objectives*. San Francisco, 1926

_____. *Spanish Voyages to the Northwest Coast of America in the Sixteenth Century.* San Francisco, 1929

_____. *Cartography of the Northwest Coast of America to the Year 1800*, 2 vols. San Francisco, 1937

Wallis, Helen. "The First English Globe: A Recent Discovery", *Geographical Journal* (117), 1951

_____. "Further Light on the Molyneux Globes", *Geographical Journal* (121), 1951

_____, ed. *Sir Francis Drake: An Exhibition to Commemorate Francis Drake's Voyage around the World, 1577 - 1580.* British Museum, 1977

_____. "The Cartography of Drake's Voyage". See Thrower, ed. *Sir Francis Drake*

_____, with Anna Maria Crinò. "New Researches on the Molyneux Globes", *Der Globusfreund,* Wein, 1987

Ward, Robert. "Drake and the Oregon Coast", *Geographical Magazine*, June 1981

_____. "Lost Harbour Found! The Truth about Drake and the Pacific", *The Map Collector*, Winter 1988

_____. "Churchill Fellowship to examine Drake's Maps", *The Map Collector*, Summer, 1992

Waters, David W. *The Art of Navigation in England in Elizabethan and Early Stuart Times*, 3rd edition. London, 1978

_____. "Elizabethan Navigation", in Thrower, ed., *Sir Francis Drake*

Weir, Alison. *Elizabeth the Queen*, London, 1998

Williamson, James A. *Sir John Hawkins, the Time and the Man.* Oxford, 1927

_____, ed., *The Observations of Sir Richard Hawkins.* London, 1933, Reprinted, Amsterdam, 1970

_____. *The Age of Drake.* London 1938. Reprinted, London, 1960

_____. *Hawkins of Plymouth.* London, 1949 and 1969

_____. *Sir Francis Drake.* London, 1951

Wilson, Derrick. *The World Encompassed.* New York, 1977